Whistling in the Dark

Whistling
in the Dark

A FOREST OF DEAN
GIRLHOOD IN THE 1940s

JOYCE LATHAM

THE LOCAL HISTORY COMPANY

For my dear cousin, Lucy Oliver,
with fondest love and sincere admiration for her very special
brand of courage and unfailing sense of humour.

First published in the United Kingdom in 1994 by
Alan Sutton Publishing Ltd · Phoenix Mill · Far Thrupp · Stroud ·
Gloucestershire

This edition first published in 2008 by
The Local History Company, an imprint of the History Press
Cirencester Road · Chalford · Gloucestershire · GL6 8PE

British Library Cataloguing in Publication Data. A catalogue record for
this book is available from the British Library

ISBN 978-07509-5037-4

Library of Congress Cataloging in Publication Data applied for

Typeset in 12/14pt Garamond.
Typesetting and origination by
The History Press
Printed and bound in England.

Contents

Acknowledgements

Once again, my sincere thanks to my dear husband, Bob, and all my close family for their patience and cooperation while this book was in progress. To all at Alan Sutton Publishing, with special thanks to John Hudson once again for his editing skills, Doug Mclean and all his staff (Forest Bookshop) for their constant warm encouragement. To my dear son, Martin, who has produced another brilliant book jacket, and to all of you who were so kind in your remarks concerning my first book – you have given me the confidence to write this one. Bless you all.

I am deeply grateful to the following for generously entrusting me with their most cherished and personal photographs. In alphabetical order: Alec Baldwin, Gladys Beddis, Winifred Blackburn, John Cox, Mrs H. Greenaway, Margaret Jenkins, Bob, Martin and Michael Latham, Anne Lewis, Wendy Pearce, John Saunders, Clive Ward, Fred Wintle.

Note from the Family

Sadly our mum, Joyce Latham, died on 27th February 2007. Her three children, Mike, Sally and Martin, would like to thank everyone who made her books a great success the first time around. We hope she will be remembered with great fondness for her lovely prose and poetry and hope those who read her books will find them inspirational. She loved life and the beautiful Forest of Dean where she lived. She never had a bad word for anyone and was great fun to be around, always making people smile and touching the lives of so many. She was a wonderful mum and friend to Mike, Sally and Martin, a precious nan to John and Paul, much loved by Lucy, Cilla and Liana, and was nanny Joyce to Jeremy and Zoe. She was very proud of her great-granddaughters Tasha, Lily, Scarlett and Ione. We all miss you so much and you will always be in our hearts. Rest in peace, the best mum anyone could ever have.

CHAPTER ONE

The New School

There were not too many passing strangers in Coleford in September 1943, and if they were there, it was as often as not by mistake. A combination of blackouts and the removal of road signs to baffle the foe made all country places hard to find, and in the Forest of Dean, with its twists and turns and wooded byways, only natives could find their way from A to B with any certainty. If there had been a newcomer to the town up on the top of Lords Hill on that early autumn morning when my friends and I started at Bell's Grammar School, he might not have been hard-pressed to understand the fear and bewilderment we felt as we passed through those big white gates for the first time. A country school in scale with a small country community; what could be more natural than for children from scattered village schools to progress to this larger institution at the age of eleven? What, indeed? But those were far from the thoughts running through our minds that morning – and if the truth be out, I confess that to my great surprise, I never did feel fully at one with Bell's Grammar School.

I was there thanks to passing a full scholarship from Christchurch School, up in that cluster of country hamlets around Berry Hill a couple of miles north of Coleford. By the time I came to secondary school age the couple I knew as my Mam and Dad – my true mother's parents – were living on a pension of 10*s* a week, and that kind of money did not run to the luxury of paying for a child to go through grammar school. Apart from having my fees paid, I qualified for a one-off grant of £3 to help buy the green and yellow Bell's uniform – with the proviso that it would have to be refunded in full if I decided to leave before the age of sixteen. What agonies that particular small print would cause me in the years ahead.

Auriel Short, a classmate at Christchurch, had also won a free scholarship, but I was not without other support on that first day at Bell's. My best friend and cousin Joyce Gwilliam was there, along with Joan Sollars, Margaret Benfield, my cousin Doreen Farr, Mervyn Hawkins and an evacuee, Janice Malloy. They had all gone through on half or entrance scholarships, which meant their parents were paying some or all of their fees, at the cost of much self-sacrifice in some cases.

On that first, strange day, we stuck together like a cowed little flock of Forest sheep – 'ship', as we'd known them all our short lives. There was so much to learn about our new environment. Christchurch had been the kind of school where older girls had been little mothers to the infants, where knots of children sat under trees to be taught on hot summer days, where one of the teachers, knowing of my family background, made a serious attempt to adopt me – though in truth my relationship with her was never nearly as cosy as that gesture might suggest. Now, at Bell's, we were faced by a building like some impressive mansion that housed the senior pupils, the headmaster's study and the staff room, and elsewhere such hitherto unknown facilities as a canteen, a physics laboratory and a large assembly hall. At least Auriel and I knew something of the long single-storey New School, since we had been there for our oral exam earlier in the year; but this was scant comfort to us as we wandered around that first day, taking stock.

We were not without help. A prefect showed us into school and pointed out our cloakroom to the left, just inside the front door. On down the corridor was our third-form classroom, and as I grew bolder I ventured on to discover the science laboratory, a long room of wide benches sinister with bunsen burners, tripods, evaporating bowls and other such paraphernalia. On shelves around the walls were dainty weighing scales with minute weights and forceps in glass cases; and everywhere there was the sickly smell of gas. That made me shudder, but though this was all a world away from Mam's kitchen and the strictly non-clinical classrooms of Christchurch, my optimism and lively curiosity ensured that no alarm bells rang in me that first day. They would be sounding soon enough, however, for this was a place I would learn to fear and hate.

There was also much to cheer us in the classroom that first day. I liked the idea of single desks, with their freedom and privacy, after

Once impressive and well-maintained, the original Bell's Grammar School building before its restoration.

the elbow-clashing intimacy of Christchurch. Ironically, there was more to see in the world beyond than at my rural primary school, where high windows cut off the view of the churchyard and the funeral processions that would have brought our work to a halt. Here at Bell's a row of tall windows looked out over playing fields, a little railway line and lovely green meadows beyond.

A bell rang, and we were led out of the school to the assembly hall for morning prayers. A prefect handed us our books and we made our way towards the front of the wide room, a little overawed by the semicircle of chairs on the stage ahead of us, with a larger one in the middle, behind a polished table. A procession of teachers in long black gowns passed us to take up their places on the platform, and the tall, slightly stooped figure of the man we were soon to learn was Mr Hough, the headmaster, was soon the focus of our attention in the central chair. As I gazed up at him, the thought struck me that his long, kindly looking face, twinkling blue eyes and fair, smooth complexion came close to God as I had always imagined him. What would he have made of such childish thoughts? It was not the Ten Commandments that came down from the stage, though; just a short speech of welcome and a few dos and don'ts. We were all feeling a little more in the swim by the time we were dismissed, and on my way back to the classroom I recognized an old friend in the form of a big Tortoise stove of the kind we'd had at Christchurch. It quite cheered me up.

What was very different from my primary school was the constant changing of teachers through the school day. I was impressed by that. There were also smells to savour, as well as sights and sounds: the pungent tang of leather from those who could afford new satchels – and the reek of Mansion Polish from my second-hand one, which Mam had rubbed strenuously to bring up the shine. Then there was the more subtle scent of new cloth. There is a theory that school uniforms are great social levellers, but the myth was soon dispelled as I took stock of my classmates. Those not so well off wore gymslips and blazers of an obviously poorer grade than those of the other girls, and our blouses were of cheaper cotton. Not that this worried me much at the time, and I found my fellow pupils a sociable, unpretentious lot.

Our class was divided into the four school houses, Raglan, Berkeley, Woodstock and Goodrich, the names of castles in our corner of the world; whichever was nearest to your home became your house, and Christchurch, English Bicknor and Lydbrook pupils fell under the umbrella of Goodrich, that fine grey ruin to the north of Symonds Yat. They soon instilled in us a fierce pride in our house as we battled for shields and cups in a variety of sporting, academic and cultural endeavours; perhaps less to the credit of the system, we also took readily to rubbishing any achievements of our competitors. Goodrich had quite a name for games, a record to which I added no lustre whatsoever. I was one of those people – who tend to be girls rather than boys – who could see no sense at all in rushing round after a stupid ball on a cold, wet field when you could be curled up somewhere snug with a good book.

The other Christchurch girls, the Lydbrook gang, they all played up for Goodrich as if they had been born for it and their lives depended on it. I was small, admittedly, but Marlene Penn was even smaller, and there was never a more keen and eager competitor in a variety of sports. It soon dawned on everyone that I was not much of an asset, a fact borne out to the full one afternoon on the hockey field. Our opponents were our arch rivals Woodstock, and the disgrace of that afternoon lives with me still. I had been put at full-back, probably because it was hoped that I would have nothing to do there, and as I stood there bored to tears, taking no interest in the game, I found the ball passed optimistically in my direction. I was beginning to lift my stick in a lackadaisical manner when I realised that a very large member of the other team was tanking down on me – and as I glanced up at that menacing figure, hockey stick held high, I lost my nerve completely. Forgetting everything but self-preservation, I flung myself from the pitch to the safety of a hedge as if it were heaven, at which the Amazonian Woodstock girl whacked the ball into the goal unopposed. The board at the back of the net rattled, and that was as good as the death knell of my sporting life.

Come summer, I thought rounders might be more my game. The captain surveyed me rather dubiously as I offered my services, but as this was not the largest school in the world, my offer was taken up. At last my turn came, and after lashing wildly at the first two balls, I connected with the third with a satisfying thwack. What I should have done then was sail round the four bases on what American baseball fans call a 'home run'. What in fact I did was let the bat fly backwards out of my hand and cosh the girl behind me square between the eyes. To my horror, she keeled over, and after all the fuss had died down I crept off to the cloakroom, my future in yet another sport in tatters. From then on, every games lesson would find me hiding somewhere with a book under my nose. All this was strictly against the rules, and they should have sent search parties out to drag me back to the thick of the fray; strange to tell, they never did.

CHAPTER TWO

The Misfit

Every two weeks our position in the form was revealed on a list
pinned to the classroom wall. At first I did fairly well,
especially in English and French, but after a while the rot set in
and I found my name sinking nearer and nearer to the bottom of
the page. Looking back, I am convinced that this was partly
because of my growing fear and dread of our science master. It was
a case of mutual loathing at first sight. He was a big man with a
fat, sneery face, squashed-in nose and steely blue eyes under bushy
brows. He had a well-earned reputation as a strict, sarcastic
disciplinarian, with the unappealing habit of tweaking small boys'
ears round and round, and the tendency to administer the whack
on the flimsiest excuse. Old Olive, the harridan of Christchurch
school – and the one who, in my later days there, improbably
wished to be my mother – seemed like a saint in comparison.

In the first week the teachers would introduce themselves to the
class, and in return we would fill in a questionnaire asking, among
much else, our father's occupation. Since my father's only deed
known to us was getting my mother pregnant with me, I always
answered this with a dash, which was quite enough for all the
teachers apart from Mr Quayle. 'What's this supposed to mean?' he
bellowed, stabbing the offending short line with his podgy finger.
In a quivering voice, I tried to explain, and the look of contempt
this earned me brought back another low point of my life, when
my family history had earned similar disapproval in an interview
with the headmistress of Monmouth High School for Girls. From
then on, the science master seemed to take the greatest delight in
picking on me for the slightest fault. In particular, he relished
sneering at my drawings of experiments in the lab; drawing was
not one of my strong points, but I sweated blood to produce
acceptable work. On one occasion he called me to the front of the
class, ripped my latest effort from my exercise book, pinned it to

Mr Quayle, the dreaded science master (front row, centre), with Mr Margerison (left) and Mr Ashworth, 'Squash', (right). Behind are four of Joyce's classmates. Left to right: Margaret Benfield, Joan Sollars, Clarice Howells, Beryl Wright.

the blackboard and offered my tittering classmates a prize if they could identify what it was supposed to be. This did nothing whatever to my very meagre stock of self-confidence, and it was not long before I began to hate the school in general and Mr Quayle in particular.

On the plus side, Miss Davis, our English teacher, was always supportive, to the extent, one day, of writing to ask Mam if it would be convenient for her to call at our home. This put her in quite a flutter since to her, teachers, like policemen and doctors, were almost on a par with royalty. Our little bungalow down Marions Lane at Berry Hill was not exactly a palace, but we had nothing to be ashamed of, and nobody could have kept the house more clean and sparkling. The decision to grant Miss Davis an audience was not an easy one for Mam to make, but she eventually agreed, and when the day came there was a kettle boiling on the hob in readiness for her arrival. With her was Sam Morgan, our geography master, a white-haired Welshman with a towering temper and a heart of gold.

They soon put Mam at her ease, and it was with far more puzzlement than anger that they declared that I was not making the progress they had hoped of me. 'According to your scholarship results you should be one of the first six in the class, Joyce,' Miss Davis said. 'Can you explain why that has not happened?'

I did not know how to answer without implicating Mr Quayle, but when they gently persisted it all came out: my fear and dislike of him and some of the reasons for those feelings. There was a long silence when my near-tearful story came to a close, and when a look of anger passed between the teachers, I realised that it was in no way directed at me.

Miss Davis changed the subject by asking where I did my homework. This seemed safer ground, and I explained that the work was always carried out on our front room table by the light of a brass oil lamp. Both teachers seemed worried about this, but I could not understand what all the fuss was about. We had never been used to electricity, having always had lamps and candles, and the same applied to thousands of Forest households. Many other Bell's pupils were in the same boat. Other than that it was a friendly and cordial visit, and they shook hands with Mam and enthused about her lovely cup of tea before wishing us goodbye. Nothing was ever said about their visit at school, but Miss Davis was extra kind and supportive of me during the rest of my time at Bell's.

But in spite of having allies in the staff room, my life at the school was never the same again after I fell foul of the science master. I knew it was a real struggle for my parents to keep me there on a 10s a week pension, and I was determined to leave as soon as I could, when I turned fourteen. Mam was driving herself into the ground, taking in other people's washing, doing it all in the back kitchen boiler and wringing everything by hand. We went blackberrying to finance the school uniform that I needed after that one-off grant of £3, selling the fruit at the Rising Sun at Five Acres for 4d a pound. It always took many hours of hard, tiring work to kit me out each September. Mam's youngest daughter and my natural mother's youngest sister, my Auntie Vi, helped out with what she could afford, and somehow or other we always just managed to get by. It worried me, having to ask Mam for extras needed at school. I can still see her dear, work-worn hands opening up her purse, and the way she would peer anxiously at the meagre contents to see whether there was enough for my needs. All in all, though not all my memories of Bell's Grammar School are unhappy, by the end of the wartime years I could not wait for March 1946, and fourteen-year-old freedom, to release me into a waiting world.

CHAPTER THREE

Take Your Partners

Though sport passed me by completely I was no slouch on the dance floor, whether it was shaking a leg to Rufty Tufty and Newcastle at Christchurch school or outdoing Ginger Rogers at village-hall hops. Those Ginger Rogers musicals with Fred Astaire; I'd wallow in their glory in the picture-house in Coleford, and twirl around my bedroom for hours, draped in an old lace curtain and with garden flowers gripped to my hair, as the gramophone played a polka or Strauss waltz. Much more in my age group was Shirley Temple – not everybody's cup of tea, but I must confess I adored her, especially in her musical moments. And then there was Carmen Miranda, with the contents of an entire chapel harvest festival on her head. Her dress sense made me wild with envy, as did her seemingly effortless dance routines. I longed to be able to sweep across those gleaming marble floors and down those stately staircases of the Hollywood films. Yes, when I grew up I, too, would be a glamorous dancer who would make the world catch its breath.

I was not on my own. In my class alone, two other girls shared similar dreams. With Margaret Osborne and Margaret Jenkins I spent many a happy dinner hour producing, directing and starring in our very own imaginary musicals. What a pity all our beautiful dreams faded as we faced up to the realities of life in a poor country community; but they gave us so much innocent pleasure while they lasted.

In our family, Auntie Vi was very much on my side in all this. Hers was a natural sense of rhythm, and she was forever giving me impromptu lessons; from her I learned the waltz, foxtrot, quickstep and several of the less complicated Old Time routines. She and her best friend Eve Ward, whose husband worked away from home, would sometimes take me dancing in English Bicknor on a Saturday night, if the weather was fine, me perched atop a cushion on the rear parcel carrier of Vi's big sit-up-and-beg bike. Most of the outward journey of a couple of miles was downward, particularly on the steep

The bottom of Chapel Hill, down which Vi would cycle to the Bicknor dances.

and curvy Chapel Hill, and I shall never know how we always managed to reach the hall in one piece. I would clutch to Vi's waist for grim death as we careered madly down the hill, swerving dangerously across the road on wide bends. Sheer momentum carried us along the next level stretch until, more by luck than judgment, Vi would execute a sharp left turn and shoot into the driveway of the hall. My skinny little legs, dangling either side of the carrier, would be shaking with fear and excitement.

After paying at the door there would then be a seemingly endless wait in the ladies' cloakroom as Vi and Eve titivated themselves. What visions they were, or supposed they were, as we eventually emerged into the hall, where some little band or other would be thumping and scraping away on stage at the far end. I particularly remember Vera and her Victorians, and Vera lives with me still: tall, snow white hair immaculately coiffured for this important engagement, long black velvet gown, violin tucked under her chin, fixed smile.

By that first Saturday night Vi had already given me a few lessons in the old-fashioned waltz – one two three, one two three – in her little kitchen, causing her poor dog to beat a hasty retreat. Stomping up and down on her uneven flagstones bore little resemblance to the prospect that now confronted me on English Bicknor's beautiful shiny floor, its polished boards sprinkled liberally with French chalk; but I managed to keep my balance during the St Bernard's waltz, and

Vi's best friend Eve Ward, a regular at the Bicknor Village Hall dances.

by the time Eve was taking me round in the veleta, I was thrilled to be dancing at last on a proper floor to a real orchestra.

Vi and Eve were bright, popular girls, and were soon besieged by would-be partners. Of course I was the reluctant wallflower, my feet itching to dance to the music, and there were times when the best I could do was find myself propelled around the floor by some stout matron or other who had taken pity on me, my eyes just about level with her bulging tum. On the other hand, it was in that hall that I had my first taste of the thrills of the Lancers – skittering round the floor, faster and faster, until the ladies' feet were off the floor and we clung to the men on either side for dear life. I was always sad when the spell was broken for the interlude, though in truth the musicians had earned their break. Standing with a plate in your hand waiting for sandwiches, cakes and soft drinks had none of the exhilaration of the dance – and worse still, I soon learned that after the break the rest of the evening passed in a flash, and all too soon it would be time for 'God Save The King' and goodnights to new-found friends in the chilly night air.

Then, of course, would follow the journey home, a very different proposition from the free-wheeling swoop down Chapel Hill. I was eleven when I first started going to those dances, and in the early days Vi always offered to let me stay on the bike and be pushed part of the way. For fear of being thought a baby I would have none of this, not least because there were always neighbours of ours to keep us company along the dark lanes, and their chatter and good-natured teasing helped the time pass quickly. It would be well past midnight by the time we reached home, but Mam would always be up for us, the old iron kettle simmering invitingly on the fire. And as I sipped my hot tea, I would regale her with tales of waltzes and veletas and handsome partners that would make that little hall in English Bicknor sound like the ballroom at the Ritz.

CHAPTER FOUR

On Parade

From the age of nine I belonged to the local branch of the St John Ambulance Brigade, which met at Christchurch School. There were about a dozen of us all told, all very keen and eager, and among the ranks were my good friends Joyce Gwilliam, Margaret Benfield and Joan Sollars, whose parents Frank and Cis were officers-in-charge. What a good and useful discipline it was, and though only one of my contemporaries took up nursing as a career, I, for one, had good cause to be thankful for having learned a few rudimentary rules.

We were taught first aid in the early months, going on to lessons in home nursing. A couple of times through the year a local GP, Dr John Battle, would visit us and test the skills we had learned; we were expected to know how to treat various fractures, apply slings, dress wounds and ease nose bleeds, while home nursing involved taking temperatures, bandaging, making beds, giving bed baths and so on. We did not take our lessons lightly – but practising on one another, we had many a laugh as the hapless 'patient' endured our amateurish administrations.

Everyone looked forward to going on parade. I loved brass bands then as I do now, and marching briskly along more or less in time with the music gave me a sense of pride and exhilaration I find hard to explain. Perhaps it's proof positive that I'm a true Forester, because the Dean is one of the great brass strongholds of southern England. I also, of course, loved dressing up, and what a smart uniform the St John girls wore: grey dress, white pinafore, head-dress, collar and cuffs, black shoes and stockings and a wide white belt. I remember one hot summer day we travelled to the Waggon Works in Gloucester for a special inspection parade on that splendid ground on which the county cricket team once played its matches in the city. Mrs Sollars had impressed on us the importance of the occasion, and Mam had done me proud:

*Joyce in her St John
Ambulance uniform
down Marion's Lane.*

my pinafore, head-dress, collar and cuffs were all dazzling white and starched to perfection.

The day was sweltering, the kind that would see today's children dressed in T-shirts and shorts at most, and a combination of that, our heavy uniforms and the excitement of the occasion made for a stressful time for many of the children on parade. We had come in by coach from all corners of Gloucestershire, and it was a day we had looked forward to; before long, however, there were children fainting, and soon there was a small procession of stretcher bearers ferrying the victims to a large – and no doubt well manned – first-aid tent. I felt equally sorry for the male officers in their thick black serge suits. They would never have lived down being borne off in a swoon, but some of them looked sorely in need of shade. Through all this the Christchurch Brigade showed up splendidly. We had made a tremendous effort with our appearance, and we all managed to stay on our feet until the parade was over and we were back in the coach downing bottles of Mrs Sollars' refreshing home-made lemonade.

It was Margaret Benfield who put her St John experience to good use in later years by becoming a nurse and eventually a Sister. She showed great aptitude for all the skills involved from the very start. As for me, I remember one occasion in particular, when I was eleven years old, when I was thankful for what knowledge I had picked up. Mam rarely complained about anything, but one morning she said that she was not feeling very well. Dad was off doing a bit of hedging for Mr Humphries at Marions Lodge, and since I was the only other person at home I took the responsibility of persuading her to go back to bed until she felt her usual self. Her bedroom was just a step away from the front room of our bungalow, and I had just gone through to the kitchen to make a cup of tea when I heard a terrible cry of pain followed by an ominous thud. Fear clawing my stomach, I rushed into the bedroom and discovered Mam face-down on the floor making strange choking noises. I somehow found the strength to turn her on her side – no mean feat, since she was a heavy person and I was small and skinny for my age. I instinctively loosened the clothing around her throat, and struggled to prop her up against the bedroom wall. Her ashen face and blue lips told me that she was suffering from a heart attack. 'Oh, Mam, please don't die,' I prayed. And at the same time, I resolved to get help.

Vi and Joyce on the wall from which Joyce screamed to Mr Sollars for help. Vi's son John is on the left.

Mr Sollars was my man. His garden ended in a tall hawthorn hedge across the lane from our front gate, and I screamed his name as loudly as I could from the top of a fairly high stone wall in front of our bungalow. He was luckily at home and in earshot, and without hesitation he pounded down his garden path and cleared the hedge with an almighty leap. He told me to run up the lane and call the doctor from the home of one of our neighbours who had a phone, and as Mrs Sollars was also on the scene by now, I knew Mam would be in the best possible hands until professional help could be summoned. Dear Dr Tandy was soon on the scene, but Mam was desperately ill in Lydney Hospital before she was eventually restored to health. I shall always be grateful for the help of our good neighbours; Mr Sollars, for the rest of his life, could never get over soaring over his hedge like that. But I also took a quiet pride in my part in the incident, and was thankful for my St John training at a time when it was needed most.

CHAPTER FIVE

The Wage Earner

My fourteenth birthday could not come quickly enough, and after counting the months to 16 March 1946, I was at last down to the weeks, and then the days. When at long last the happy day dawned, I flew down Lords Hill from Bell's Grammar School with never a backward glance. The realization that I would never again have cause to fear Mr Quayle, the science master, did not dawn instantly, but when it did I felt as free as a bird. It was as if an aching burden had been lifted from my soul. What did upset me was the feeling that I had let the family down. They had expected such a lot from my winning the scholarship, and given me their wholehearted support; but for all the good it had done, I might as well have joined the vast majority of my old Christchurch schoolmates at the secondary school at Five Acres. I am sure I would have been much happier there.

I had been home for just over a week when Vi told us of a job being advertised in a small grocery shop just across the road from Marions Lane. I had always fancied the idea of working in a shop, with visions of myself as a white-clad model of efficiency, courtesy and expertise, nonchalantly weighing up butter, lard and marge, and cutting swathes through cooked meat on a bacon slicer while totting up the customers' bills. Mam must not have seen me in quite this light, since she seemed to be against the idea; but as usual, I got my own way, and when I presented myself to the shopkeeper he told me I could start the following Monday morning at 8.30 sharp. That was one of those nervy weekends, alternating between excitement and self-doubt, and it was with mixed feelings that I took my first steps in the working world that springtime Monday morning. Let us say that the job specification was not quite what I had had in mind. Far from serving in the shop, I found myself as a maid of all work for the grocer and his family, sweeping the kitchen, making the beds and – horror of

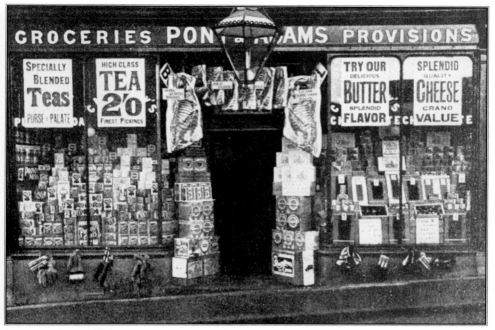

Shopping memories of Coleford: Pont and Adams' grocery shop.

horrors – emptying their smelly chamber pots into a white enamel bucket, which I then carried into the back yard and swished down a drain. After washing my hands, I hasten to add, I was also expected to wait on table and help prepare the meals at a café they owned half-way down Rock Pitch, almost directly below Symonds Yat Rock. I let Vi know all about this, and of course she told Mam, who was furious. I think she was hurt, too. She had been in service, as had my mother Elsie, and after my grammar school education she took a dim view of my doing a job that added up to very much the same kind of thing. 'Look 'ere, our Joyce, I don't want tha ta go emptying other people's jerries,' she said. 'Give in thee notice, and look vur zummat else.' I was not sorry to take her advice. The work was not for me, and I was scarcely turning my back on a fortune at 5s a week. In truth, my bosses did not seem heartbroken, either; one way and another, it was not the most auspicious start to my working life.

Coleford Market Place in the early 1930s, when the paper shop Joyce worked in was the Red and White booking office on the left.

Not long afterwards, a friend told me of a job going at the Red and White paper shop in Coleford, six days a week, starting with a paper round at 7 a.m., working until 6 p.m., but with Thursday afternoon off. Mam deemed this a more suitable calling for a former grammar school girl, and the people running the shop appeared duly impressed, too, when I went down for an interview. Having a Bell's education, however brief, seemed to give me the edge over other applicants, and again the job was mine. I still used the small bike Mam had bought second-hand a couple of years previously; by this time I must have looked like a tom-tit on a pump handle on it, but it would do until I could afford a new one, and it certainly stood me in good stead that first morning, getting me to the shop with a good five minutes to spare after a 6.45 start. Two young ladies were already busy sorting the papers into piles, and as we were all from the Berry Hill area, I soon found myself at ease with them. One, Dorothy Short, was not too much older than I was, and lived a couple of doors down from my first place of work. Betty, the elder one, took charge of the shop when our boss,

*Drapers, milliners, purveyors of linoleums: the old-time shops of Coleford
served a population for whom a trip to Gloucester was a considerable
undertaking.*

Mr Turner, was away – but he was there that morning, sorting out
a big canvas bag for my paper round and handing me my book
with customers' names, addresses and paper and magazine orders.
Betty showed me how to name and number the orders and pack
them neatly in the bag, after which I was on my own.

That bag was heaving at the seams and almost dragging along
the ground by the time I had filled it, and the straps bit into my
shoulders as I toiled up Cinderhill and High Nash and then off left
along Tufthorn Avenue with its long garden paths and fractious
dogs. I was done for by the time I had slotted the last paper
through the last letter box. My thin shoulders were aching from
the weight – but what a relief to know that the first part of my
morning's work had been achieved without mishap, and at least it
was downhill back to the shop in the middle of town. Back at the

shop I was given a green overall to wear, and there was a welcome cup of tea from Mrs Turner before I took up my duties behind the counter. I was initiated into the mysteries of giving change, but, happily, mental arithmetic was one of my strong points, and I was soon serving customers with confidence, and totting up their bills in my head. The till in that shop was just a drawer – and even the most sophisticated cash registers of that time did not do the addition for you; I wonder how many of today's cashiers would cope without those marvellous checkout machines.

My first morning flew by, crammed with so much to learn, and by 1 p.m. I was quite thankful to make my way home to lunch on my bike, accompanied up towards Berry Hill by Dorothy and Betty. There was not a lot of time to spare in the hour, but after a boiled egg and a couple of cups of tea I was able to fill Mam in on my progress to date. At least the return trip into town was quick, easy and downhill almost all the way.

The part of the job I liked most was weighing out toffees, boiled sweets and my favourite chocolate macaroons from the glass showcase in a corner of the shop. I was taught how to work out the sweet coupons for each item, and the tidy way to fasten the three-cornered paper bags that were used in those days. As for those macaroons, I must confess that not every one left the shop in exchange for cash and coupons; I couldn't resist them, and my craving sometimes got the better of my conscience when the coast was clear. One of my chores was to dust the shelves once a week, and Betty could be a tartar if she discovered some speck I had overlooked. Apart from being thin, I was perhaps a bit thin-skinned, too, and a sarcastic remark from her could reduce me to tears. Dorothy was more easy-going; we had many a laugh together, and all in all, I was quite happy in my new job. My wages were 10s a week, out of which I kept half a crown and gave Mam 7s 6d. I was beginning to take more interest in my appearance by now, and a shilling of that weekly half-crown went into a clothing club run by one of Mam's friends – leaving me a grand total of 1s 6d to spend as I wished.

I had started at the paper shop in the summer of 1946, and as winter approached I began to find my morning delivery round a great deal less inviting. Sometimes I returned to the shop and discovered that some other paper boy or girl had found the prospect of a dark, rainy morning even less inviting than I had, and had failed to turn in. It would then be a quick cup of tea and off on my bike again, perhaps as far afield as Newland and Clearwell – until the day came, early in 1947, when even the newspapers failed to turn up. It was an episode that none of us around at the time will ever forget.

CHAPTER SIX

The Big Freeze

For days the skies had been dull, and heavy with banks of grey cloud. We had not given this much thought; after all, we had got through January and February without mishap, and come March our thoughts were turning towards spring. And yet, and yet . . . Could it be that old man winter still had a trick or two up his sleeve? 'I dunno what's the matter wi' thoy bloomin' cats lately,' Mam mused. 'I con't zeem ta get um ta muv from the vire.'

At 6.15 a.m. my little Smith's alarm woke me as usual for work. I fumbled for matches to light my candle, and thought in a distracted way that it seemed oddly dark and quiet outside my window. The birds were obviously having a lie-in. As I dressed I heard Mam moving around the house – and it was when she opened our kitchen door that I heard her gasp of 'Oh, good Gawd!'. I rushed through, and in the flickering candlelight I rocked back on my heels at the sight of a towering wall of snow cutting us off from the outside world. It was the same story at the front door – snow the like of which I had never seen before, snow straight from books of fairytales from Iceland and Norway.

Our kitchen fire was out, and we were bitterly cold. Mam scraped out the dead ashes as I held a candle, and it was not long before the old iron kettle was simmering again. We always kept our morning wood drying in the oven overnight, plus a few logs on the hearth, and over and above this we had one or two knobs of coal left over from the day before. When Dad struggled out of the bedroom to see what all the fuss was about, Mam sent him back. He was far too weak to do anything, and was told firmly that he would be more help keeping out of the way in his warm bed than coughing and wheezing in our chilly kitchen. Between us, Mam and I somehow managed to burrow our way to the back kitchen in an outhouse, where a long-handled coal shovel was just what we needed to dig a narrow path through the snow to our outside lavatory. Our little dog Peggy rushed out for her usual morning run around the garden – and then stopped dead in her tracks, overawed by this new experience. Snow blocked the windows and filled the lane to the top of the hedgerow. Another of our daily rituals, fetching water from the spring well, was obviously out of the question, but we felt there was no real problem here; when you are 8 ft deep in snow, you can scarcely complain of being in danger of dying of thirst. Nevertheless, the chore of shovelling snow in a tin bucket and melting it on the fire was surprisingly time-consuming. A full pail of snow yielded very little water, and the process had to be repeated several times before we had enough to fill the kettle and a small bowl for washing. We had a small stock of coal and logs in the back kitchen, but not knowing when the next loads could be delivered, we felt the need to be very sparing with fuel. 'It might be a vew days before we get the next lot,' said Mam. This turned out to be one of her more over-optimistic pronouncements; as all who recall those times will know, it was weeks and weeks before life got back to normal again.

The start of the heavy snows at Five Acres during that remarkable winter of early 1947.

After the snow came a biting frost, then down would come another fall, followed by a yet more severe freeze. The drifts took on the appearance of layered cake, and life moved slowly and uncertainly. When people of my generation look back on severe winters, it is the early months of 1947 and 1963 that come most readily to mind; but the big freeze of '63 was not notable for its heavy snowfalls – 'It's too cold to snow,' people used to grumble – and for sheer drifts-up-to-the-eaves spectacle, no winter since has ever matched 1947.

Our good neighbours up the lane realized our predicament, and banded together to dig a narrow path to our bungalow. I struggled through this to Kay's shop to buy one or two essentials, and was surprised to find that several of the assistants had been able to turn in. They did a good job ensuring that everything was shared out fairly, and no customer was left without a few candles, matches, paraffin or tinned milk, as well as the usual rations of fats, tea, sugar and so on. Bread was delivered by sledge, and the milkmen also found means of slithering around to visit us, but there were no newspapers, and the fact that we lived in the heartland of Gloucestershire's mining industry was of no avail; there was no chance of the coal merchants' horse-drawn drays passing down our little lane. What we did have was the all-pull-together spirit that had recently brought us through the hardships of war, and that counted for a lot until life returned to normal.

We saw winter in all its beauty and harshness. The frost patterns on the window panes, icicles like Clearwell Cave stalactites, the undulating sculpture of drifting snow, the sheer, striking awesomeness of a landscape of glittering silver as far as the eye could see, roads and hedgerows whitewashed from the face of the earth . . . On the other hand, old trees succumbed to the weight of snow, and for the farmers and sheep badgers (Foresters who kept a small flock to supplement their wages) there was the hardship of a lambing season like none they had ever known. Many ewes were dug out dead, some with their new-born lambs – but as always there were the stories of survival against seemingly insuperable odds, and all manner of tales of heroism, human and animal, began to circulate the Forest as, inch by inch, we clawed our way back to normality.

It was some days before I ventured out to work in Coleford again. There was a huge drift on the top of Gorse Hill, and all you could see of the almshouses was the bedroom windows and roofs. Gangs of men armed with shovels and spades had brought some sanity back to the town centre, with the roads passable and narrow paths cut along the pavements to the shops. There were still no newspapers in town, however, and Mr Turner told me not to struggle in again until the thaw had set in. That made sense – but, of course, this would be a strictly unpaid holiday. For that reason and many others, the thaw could not come quickly enough, and we felt a battle had been won when the papers and post began to trickle through again. With the sunshine came the added misery of flooding, and it was several weeks before our little world was back to normal again. What was striking, down our lane, was the absence of many a stout stake in the hedgerow, uprooted to eke out some family's meagre supply of fuel. Anti-social? I suppose so, but I confess that I had hoiked a few out myself when the crisis was at its peak. The war-time spirit, after all, was a cunning mixture of community action and self-preservation when the going got tough.

The rear of the King's Head, Coleford, almost hidden by the snows of 1947.

First Snowfall

Stealthy snowflakes blowing in the wind
Drift softly over branches stark and bare,
And soon a vestment, sugar-spun, hides Nature's nakedness.

The crackling bracken bows beneath its weight,
Then disappears from view.
Familiar scenes and landmarks are erased, and in their place
A miracle of flowing shapes of virgin white
   excites the eye.

When night frosts breathe across this alien land,
We walk through glistening diamonds, ankle-deep,
And even humble grasses wear tiaras.
Grey guttering beneath the old barn roof
Festooned in gleaming stalactites of ice
Shimmers like crystal chandeliers.

All sound is muted,
Locked in Nature's spell.
Winter's white magic – first snowfall.

CHAPTER SEVEN

Music –
and the Babysitter

Auntie Vi was the proud possessor of a handsomely carved walnut piano, and could play well enough. Pianos were a familiar sight in so many parlours, then, and it was by no means unusual to take music lessons. I loved to sit quietly and listen as Vi practised the latest song from sixpenny sheet music with its cover adorned by some romantic scene and a portrait of the singer or band leader who had made it popular.

My friends Joyce Gwilliam and Joan Sollars were doing well under the tuition of Pam Chandler, a lovely young woman who was expert as a musician and as patient as you could imagine. She certainly needed to be when Vi persuaded Mam that it would be a good idea if I took lessons, too. As we had no piano, Vi let me practise on hers, and while I was never a great one for scales, I was thrilled when I mastered my first small piece of music. I played that tune over and over again, and must have set poor Vi's teeth on edge. By the time I was twelve I had progressed to Strauss waltzes. At first I had difficulty in spanning an octave with my small hands, but Pam's encouragement ensured that I succeeded after a while.

Unfortunately for the world of the arts, my musical career began to go awry when Vi and her husband Eric produced their son John. Their front room was directly under the little one's bedroom, and my strumming on the piano every day was obviously out of the question. Pam kindly offered me the use of hers when it was not needed by her many pupils, but since her father worked shifts at the pit, there were times when it was not convenient. After a while I decided there was no future in my continuing with the piano, and like many another of my generation, I wish I had gone on with it; it was certainly not for lack of support from dear Pam and her mother.

Auntie Vi with her children Wendy and John.

At one time Vi and her family lived next door to Charlie Kay's shop in Berry Hill, close to the King's Head. I spent much of my time there, playing with her daughter Wendy and later helping with little John. He was one of the happiest little chaps you could wish to find, with his mum's bright red hair and blue eyes. I was twelve when he was born, Wendy seven, so I was deemed old enough to take him for walks in his brand new pram, give him a bottle and generally keep an eye on him. One job I always managed to wise out of was changing his nappy, making myself scarce when that particular operation seemed imminent.

Occasionally I would babysit when Vi and Eve went to those dances in Bicknor on Saturday night. They were both young mothers, for Eve, who lived across the road, had three children – Clive, Roger and little Anne. Her husband was away in the RAF.

John was always in bed by 6 p.m., so Wendy and I would be told to tiptoe round the house, playing as quietly as possible. We kept this up until Vi and Eve disappeared, by which time Wendy would also be in bed; but she was never asleep, and as soon as we had the house to ourselves we'd let rip and have the time of our lives, playing the rowdiest games while dear little John slept on in the next room. A beautiful blue silk eiderdown covered Wendy's bed, and we'd drag it on to the floor and dive off the mattress into it, pretending it was the sea. At other times I would make a throne from the pillows, drape the eiderdown around Wendy's shoulders and plonk John's Bakelite potty on her head as a crown. The bed was her golden coach, and I would be the driver, jumping up and down on the creaking springs until she fell off her perch and we both collapsed in giggles. I was always crafty enough to tidy up before settling down to sleep in Wendy's bed, and Vi never did realize what we had been up to. Not that it ever caused John any trouble; he simply snoozed through it all.

Sometimes my services as a babysitter were required by my real mother, Elsie. As an occasional treat, her husband Bill would take her to the first house at the pictures in Coleford on a Saturday afternoon, and I would be asked to take charge of little Margaret, Billy and Eileen; John and Yvonne had yet to be born. I always felt very important when asked to do this job, quite the little mother,

*Three of Joyce's half-siblings
– John, Eileen and Yvonne
in 1950.*

and saw bathing them as one of my foremost duties. Amid loud
protests, I would fill a large saucepan with water, heat it on their
kitchen range, and drag their big zinc bath from the back kitchen
to the hearth. Making the children stand well back, I would then
somehow tip the heavy panful of hot water into the bath, following
it with a bowl of cold. Then I'd test the temperature with my
elbow, as I'd seen Vi do, and by the time Elsie and Bill returned
home, their kitchen would be awash with soapy water, as were my
clothes. The little ones would be in various stages of undress,
screaming at the carbolic soap in their eyes, and everyone's hair was
in a soap-suddy, matted mess. I felt really hurt when I realized that
my earnest efforts were appreciated by nobody, parents or children.

In due course, Vi's youngsters Wendy and John passed for Bell's
Grammar School, and made a far more positive impression than I
ever had, especially in games. Wendy shone at running, vaulting,
the long-jump, hockey and tennis. John was also an all-rounder,

*A sporty type: Vi's daughter Wendy high-jumping at
Bell's Grammar School.*

excelling at football. Perhaps the fact that he used to eat four
Shredded Wheat for breakfast, long before the advertising men had
caught on to the idea, had something to do with his prowess; he
was certainly never short of energy.

Their father Eric owned a small pleasure boat at Symonds Yat,
powered by a pair of oars and plenty of muscle. Every weekend
through the summer he could be found rowing trippers back and
forth along the river between the Saracen's Head and Whitchurch
Ferry, and while both he and his brother Narn made a little extra
money from this, it was hard-earned. At other times he would act
as a ghillie for visiting toffs wishing to do a spot of salmon fishing.
He had been brought up at Doward and knew the Wye like the
back of his hand, but I suspect that not all his wealthy clients (or
indeed, Eric and co.) were operating with the benefit of fishing
rights.

Like a lot of the men of the river, Eric had quite a thirst, and
he'd always be keen to have a few bob put aside for his drink.

A beauty in the making: Vi in her younger days.

Often in their early married life he'd return home to the house they shared with his mother in Doward in the evening complaining of a slack day's work, until Vi began to wonder whether he was not being just a little economical with the truth. One morning, after waving him goodbye, she cut a pile of sandwiches, brewed a flask of tea and put them in a carrier bag along with a strong pair of binoculars. Crossing over on the ferry, she remarked casually to the operator that she was going to visit Mam at Whippingtons Brook, an out-of-the-way spot we once lived in not far from Christchurch Cross. But her real destination was the top of Symonds Yat Rock, from which she looked down on the Wye until late afternoon, watching Eric putting in a busy day's work carrying passengers to and fro.

Come tea time he trudged home, and Vi asked him pleasantly whether trade had been good. 'Nothing much, love – only a few little trips,' he replied in his usual care-worn way. He didn't know what had hit him when Vi went for him like a raging tiger, giving a detailed account of all his comings and goings that day. He must have thought she had a crystal ball hidden away somewhere – but whatever, he never tried that trick again.

The Order of the Bath

Zum folks love ta brag about thoyr shower an' bathroom suite,
If they ain't got a bidet, thoyr lives won't be complete.
'Moin's all in apple green,' thoy drool, 'wi' bath set in the floor,'
An' zum on um got plastic plants a'clomberin' up the door,
Wi' matchin' towels an' flannels, too, an' proper bathroom mats,
Huge mirrors plonked around the place, an' queer-shaped
   shower 'ats.
It looks like summat theese could vind in them Arabian Nights,
Complete wi' perfumed oils an' soaps, an' softly shaded lights.

Oi think o' 'ow it used ta be when Vriday noight cum round,
A gurt zinc bath afore the vire in our 'ouse could be vound,
Surrounded by a cleanish bit o' sackin' vur our vit,
Just like our Vurest miners 'ad, when thoy cum wum vrum pit.
Two saucepans vull 'o rainwater vrom our old outzide tank,
Now noicely warm, were emptied in, while all our zpirits zank.
Then one by one – or two by two, according ta the size,
Mam dumped us in, an' scrubbed awoy, ignorin' all our cries.
The tail o' Faither's ol' striped shirt, cut roughly ta a
   square,
Were smot in red carbolic zoap, afore we was aware.
Her'd twist thick flannel in our ears, an up each nostril, too,
Vrom dirty lug 'oles, zo 'er zed, great green-stemmed taters
   grew.
Shampoo were never 'eard of, then, carbolic did the trick,
Thouse quickly learned ta shut thee chops – zoap zwallowed
   made tha sick.
The bit I really hated most, an' think o' still wi' dread
Were when 'er poured cold water on me unzuzpectin' yud.
But then at last 'er'd lift us out, ta ztand afor thic vire,
'Er'd rub us wi' a rough ol' towel, and cause us ta perzpire.
Aye, though we 'ad no bathroom posh, wi' zuite o' apple green,
When Man an' Faither's shirt were done, o' butty, we waz
   CLEAN.

CHAPTER EIGHT

Stepdad Bill

I was about a year old when my natural mother Elsie married a near neighbour, Bill Sollars, and went to live in his family home in Hillersland Lane, a stone's throw from where we then lived at the Barn House. He was always very kind to me, as were all his folks. On the surface he was quiet, kindly and unassuming, never one to raise his voice in anger, content with his lot, and with the dry wit of a true Forester. His appearance fitted his inoffensive manner – short, balding and with mild, short-sighted eyes peering from behind thick lenses, and it was only after his death a couple of years ago, at the grand old age of ninety-three, that another side of his character was revealed to me.

A miner for most of his life, Bill hardly ever mentioned his army days in the First World War, but in the last few years of his life he decided to record some of his experiences in a book, with the help of his sister Winnie Blackburn. From it I learned that he had been a member of the Royal Warwickshire Regiment, serving in Britain, France and Belgium. He was awarded a cross guns insignia for his work in the essential though much disliked role of a sniper, and was later put in charge of five men operating a Lewis gun. Both duties were highly dangerous, but Bill came through them unscathed. Only he knew how often he relived the horrors imprinted in his mind.

Bill's front room was full of family heirlooms handed down through the years. A large stag's head with mighty antlers watched your every move through glassy eyes, various tall vases and ornaments crowded the mantelpiece, and everywhere dark pictures and photographs added their own contribution to the story of his forefathers. His prize possessions were on either side of a finely carved upright piano – two dainty stuffed red squirrels, each in his separate case and crouched on small branches in an identical pose. Both held a hazelnut between their sharp front teeth – and

Bill Sollars at the Front.

hazelnuts being food, I suppose it was inevitable that my curiosity should get the better of me.

One day the little ones were playing in the garden, Bill and Elsie were leaning over their gate in animated conversation with a neighbour, and I found myself alone in the room with the squirrels. A chair on one side of the piano provided easy access to one of the cases and I quickly clambered up. I was surprised that the glass panel slid open quite easily, and almost before I knew what I was doing, I was pushing my inquisitive little fingers into the creature's jaws. Heart beating furiously, I gave the hazelnut a sharp tug – and out it flew, along with several of the squirrel's sharp little white teeth. Scared out of my wits at the enormity of my crime, I nearly fell off the chair in my haste to make a getaway. With no thought of goodbyes, I high-tailed it quietly through the back door and home to Mam.

I was too ashamed to confess to her and hugged my guilty secret to myself, finding all kinds of excuses to get out of visiting Elsie and Bill. In the end Mam grew frustrated, and insisted that I went down on some errand or another. Nothing was mentioned when I first arrived, and I was just beginning to feel confident and comfortable when Bill pounced.

'Hey, our Joyce, coust thee remember seein' anybody a'messin' wi' one o' thoy red squirrels when thee's cum down t'other wick, o' butt?' I must have turned bright red from the neck up as I shook my head, but there was a mischievous gleam from behind his thick lenses when he said: 'Oh, well, I'd aim it must 'ave bin thick there naughty Mr Nobody agyun, weren't it, Joycee?' My dear sister Margaret delights in reminding me of this little episode almost every time we meet.

When he wasn't keeping bees, making wine, gardening or fishing in the Wye, Bill could be found tinkering with his beloved Model T Ford car. Model Ts were not the grandest of grand – but cars were so thin on the ground around our way that to own one at all was a tremendous status symbol. Bill made his work for its living by hiring it out occasionally, and although we kids were not allowed to poke about in the garage, I must confess I managed to peep in on it once or twice. It seemed huge to me, with its brass lamps and radiator, and I am sure a Model T would not change hands at economy prices today. As I said, hardly any working people had cars in those days, and the fact that Bill did showed his determination to go for a goal and attain it. With the same resolution, he would cycle all the way to Lydney to learn to drive from Mr Watts, who then owned a small garage. From that business has grown a very large concern indeed, and the family today is well known and respected throughout the Forest. Not that all Bill's thoroughness was directed towards self-improvement. When Dad became too ill to tend our big garden, Bill was the son-in-law who would find time, amid all his other activities, to come up and help us out. He was always so kind and supportive, and my Mam and Dad could not have been more fond of him, or made him more welcome. In later years, Bill always made sure that my husband Bob and I, and our three children, were never left out of any family get-togethers. He might have been small in stature, but he was a real man with a very big heart.

The Long Search

Deep in the depths of a derelict mine
Where day becomes night, and the sun cannot shine,
Mouldering pit props decay in the gloom
And silence lies brooding round that ancient tomb.
Yet somehow I know if I go there I'll find
Echoes from life's passing souls left behind.
Away in the distance men's voices I'll hear
Then small points of light in the dark will appear
With tramping of boots, and the snatch of a song
As yesteryear's miners come marching along.
Their safety lamps shine on the crumbling wall,
But men passing by leave no shadow at all,
Like Will o' the wisps they move on without trace
Eager to start one more shift at the face.
Then silence descends like a curtain once more
Until down the dramroad I hear the trucks roar,
Black tunnels vibrate as each convoy clanks by
Yet though I look hard, ne'er a one can I spy.
Machinery rusts where abandoned it stands,
Perhaps now attended by skeleton hands.
Out here in the sunshine I shiver with cold
When I think of the miners' long search for black gold.
Our coal tips are levelled, our miners have gone,
But maybe – just maybe – down there they live on.

CHAPTER NINE

Doctors and Curses

Mam had long since stopped sleeping with Dad in the big front bedroom. He often grumbled about it, but the hours of darkness had become a nightmare for us; not only was his dreadful coughing keeping us awake, but he was forever up and down going to the toilet. It was a tight squeeze for Mam and me in my little single bed. She was big, and it was a good job that I was 'one of Pharaoh's lean kine', as she was fond of saying; somehow we managed to snatch a few hours' sleep of a night, off and on.

I had to walk to Coleford once a week for Dad's medicine, up to Dr Lippiatt's surgery at Cinderhill, a little out of town. He had a cold, cheerless waiting room at the best of times, and in winter it was freezing. The good doctor spent a lot of time with each patient, so you always knew that you were in for a long wait. Before he grew too ill to leave the house, Dad collected his own medicine, and one evening he came home in a towering rage:

'I'd bin quat in thic bloody waitin' room fer a couple o' hours, gettin' colder an' colder, wi' a lot o' snifflin', keckin' buggers vull o' germs, humped over thic one, snotty gas flame. Me backside 'ad got cramp avore it were my turn to zee ol' Lippiatt. As I scrobbled dru' the door the vust thing 'im zed were "Sit down, Mr Farr." "Zit down? Zit down be buggered," I zed. "I been quat in thic bloody ice box o' thine vur a vew hours already, Doctor, zo if it be all the zame ta thee, I'd rather stand."'

Mam was horrified to think of the doctor being spoken to in such a fashion, but Dad was never much of a respecter of persons. He often told, with great relish, of his first encounter with Mrs Wyndham Jones, wife of the new vicar at Christchurch: 'I were strolling past the Vicarage, an' I zid her bent over in the gyarden, doin' a bit o' weedin' or zummat. 'Er skirt were right up around 'er backside, an' I 'ad me eyeful, I con tell tha. "Hey missus," I shouted. "Them be a lovely pair o' legs thee's got on tha." 'Er turned round grinnin' 'er yud off. "Well, thank you very much," 'er zed. "That's the nicest compliment I've had for a long time."'

From that day on, with one notable exception, neither would hear a bad word said of the other, and they would often exchange a spot of spicy banter when their paths crossed. Mrs Wyndham, as she was known, was no conventional vicar's wife. Always smart in lipstick, rouge, flashy rings and the latest fashions, she had a dominant personality that swept all before her in a frenzy of new ideas and enthusiasms. I almost became the victim of one of her brainwaves when I was working in the paper shop shortly after leaving school. She sent word by Dad that she wanted to see me at the Vicarage as soon as possible, and much intrigued, I found myself walking up her path a few evenings later.

'How would you like to live in New Zealand, my dear?' was her opening gambit; and without waiting for an answer, she told me of a young doctor friend of hers who was looking for a suitable young girl to be nursemaid to his baby. When the child was big enough for school, I would then become his receptionist. She painted a glowing picture of my prospects, and of the fine life awaiting me in New Zealand. It sounded wonderful to me, and I was happy to agree to go with her to St Briavels to meet the doctor, his wife and my little charge to be. Before I could blink we were bowling over there in her little car, and once at the house, things could hardly have gone better. I took to the doctor and his wife, they took to me, the baby was a little darling, and I was offered the job on the spot. Dazzled and bewitched, I agreed to sail with them in a month's time.

I bathed in Mrs Wyndham's approval all the way home, and could hardly wait to tell Mam and Dad. I stayed on Cloud Nine for quite a while, thinking and talking of nothing but the rosy future in store for me, but although Dad asked a few pertinent questions, Mam had very little to say. She came up with nothing to discourage me, but it was clear that she was not entering into the spirit of the venture. One evening a couple of weeks before I was due to sail we were sitting in our little front room, Mam and Dad on either side of the fireplace, our little dog Peggy curled up on Mam's home-made peg rug on the hearth and with me on my wooden stool, reading as usual. I happened to glance across at Mam, who was sitting quietly, staring into the fire, her hands folded on her ample lap as the flames sent shadows flickering and dancing round the room; and it was then, with a sudden clutch of my fourteen-year-old heart, that I realized that if I went away I would almost certainly never see her again. There I would be, on the other side of the world among strangers, while poor old Mam would be left to cope with Dad and everything else as best she could. How could I ever have been so selfish and thoughtless? What peace of mind would I have, knowing that she might be missing and needing me?

All the love and gratitude I felt for her swept over me like a tidal wave. I reached out and gripped those rough, work-worn hands, hands that could be so gentle whenever I was ill or in need of comfort. She glanced up at me, startled out of her reverie, as I said: 'I can't go, Mam. I don't ever want to leave you. Mrs Wyndham will just have to find somebody else.' Tears streamed down my face and I sobbed and sobbed, my head on her knee. It had been a harder decision to make than when, a few years earlier, I had been asked to choose between Mam and Dad and the teacher who had wished to adopt me. But after my mind had been made up the sense of relief, and of coming home, was just as tangible. Mam clutched me to her, wiping my tears in her pinafore, while Dad jumped up and stomped around cursing the young doctor and even his sparring partner Mrs Wyndham for filling my head with 'a load o' nonsense'.

There was still the not inconsiderable matter of breaking the news to the vicar's wife, but here again, Dad took control. 'Doesn't thee worry, our Joyce, I'll sort her out, all right. Thee bisn't a'goin' anywhere thee don't want to, o' butt.' True to his word, he went along with me to see her the next day; she was not at all pleased to hear my news, and I could see that I was crossed off her list from that moment on, but I felt as light as air as we walked back up the Vicarage path. Free of her spell, I could settle down to life once more with my loving Mam and Dad in the only place I felt at home, our lovely Forest of Dean.

My Lady

She never wore fine linen, or gracious velvet gowns,
The dresses that she did possess were mostly hand-me-downs.
No precious gems adorned her hands, just one plain band of
  gold,
But no fine lady in the land more love in them could hold.

No portrait painters flattered her, her beauty lay within,
And sumptuous creams and powders were strangers to her skin.
She never bothered hairdressers, although her hair was neat:
Wound in two plaits around her head, it smelled so fresh
  and sweet.

She didn't talk in accents 'posh', – broad Vurest ruled her
  speech
Yet no grand cultured gentleman more common sense could teach.
Her simple faith, her gentle heart, her tender, loving ways
Made our dear Mam the lady I shall cherish all my days.

CHAPTER TEN

Basic Needs

In common with many other rural areas in the 1940s, the Forest of Dean was a world away from the era of 'all mod cons'. Electricity and water supplies were enjoyed only by the townsfolk and people living close to main roads. We had neither; our washing and bathing were done in rainwater caught in two corrugated zinc tanks, via the roof and guttering. All our drinking water was fetched daily from a spring well quite a distance from our bungalow down a long, winding path through a neighbouring wood; our lavatory was a bucket in a hut at the bottom of the garden; we cooked on a kitchen range, and light came from oil lamps and candles in winter and the sun in summer.

The bigger of the two water tanks, beside our kitchen door and directly opposite our back kitchen, was conveniently placed for Mam's weekly wash. The other, at the side of the bungalow, was used only in emergencies – the odd dry spell in summer – to boost the dwindling level of its much-used mate. Both were raised up on layers of bricks high enough for a bucket to be slipped beneath a tap at the bottom. After a couple of days' hard frost, the water would freeze solid to quite a depth, and Dad would stand on my little three-legged stool to chip away at the ice with a hammer. I don't know how they salvaged enough water for Mam to do her washing on those occasions. Summer posed different problems. Dipping a hand bowl into the soft rainwater then would always result in its re-emerging full of tiny, wriggling, revolting creatures of unknown species. It was like washing your face in a stagnant pond. Even through the winter months, Mam insisted that we should use the back kitchen when we washed our faces in the morning. It was quite an ordeal, having to face a bowlful of cold water with lumps of ice floating around on the surface. Dad's old striped flannel shirts were in great demand as face flannels, while the bench that served as our wash stand was also the old pig bench, on which the beast was slaughtered each year. Next to the bowl lay a big lump of red carbolic soap. I'd dip the square of flannel into that icy water, smother it in soap and then, very gingerly, introduce it to my reluctant face. I always kept my eyes screwed up tight through this operation, bearing in mind how carbolic made your eyes sting. By the time all the soap was swilled off you could guarantee to be wide awake, no matter how sleepy you had been to start with.

Every Friday night would find Mam dragging our big tin tub into the kitchen in readiness for my weekly bath. Dad was banished to the front room and a clean hessian sack would be spread across the floor. Mam would put the bath on it, in front of a roaring fire on which there would be bubbling two iron kettles and a big saucepan of water between them. A big bowl of cold water went into the bath first, and then the rest. In my younger days Mam would be there, sleeves rolled up, carbolic-soaped flannel at the ready, and I would be given a good going-over. No portion of me escaped her attentions, especially my neck and lugholes. Then came the part I dreaded most; my long hair would be saturated, and carbolic would be rubbed in and soaped up to a frothy lather. Jugs of clean, lukewarm water would then be poured over to rinse – but while my hair hung over my face like a veil, Mam would sometimes slip in a jug of ice cold water, to ensure that all the soap had been rinsed off. Another hazard was the fact that the side of the bath nearest to the fire could burn you, while the other was stone cold in winter. I learned to sit in the middle, like a little island, coming in contact with neither left nor right. After my bath I would stand on the sacking while Mam dragged the tub out of the way. She would then give me a vigorous rub with a rough old towel – after all of which, if nothing else, I was well and truly clean.

There were no fairies at the bottom of our garden – only a small hut containing a lavatory bucket. The business end of this, at least, would be kept scrupulously clean, with the wooden seat scrubbed whiter than white, the walls limewashed every spring, and on the dirt floor would be a piece of sacking or a spare oilcloth. Often the Forest privvies would be 'two-holers' – one for adults and a smaller one for children; and always behind the door, on a piece of string, would be a wad of old newspaper cut into manageable squares. Only the really rich or snobbish aspired to toilet paper. Here was a place for quiet meditation, and I always took the chance to indulge in my favourite pastime of reading – not least the unkindly harsh but always absorbing squares of magazines. This could also, of course, be a frustrating form of reading, with the final paragraphs of interesting articles ripped away with abandon.

Though much cleaning went on around the business end of the privvy, all kinds of little creatures made their homes in the roof and cracked walls: woodlice, caterpillars, moths, earwigs, horse flies, bluebottles, house flies – and of course spiders, whose webs festooned every corner. Inevitably, whenever I happened to be in, the biggest, hairiest, most beady-eyed of the species would descend from the roof to perform an aerial ballet before my hypnotized gaze. Black beetles and workaholic ants scurried about their business across the floor, and moths would show an interest if you were unlucky enough to need a night visit, armed with a home-made lantern of a candle or comp in a jamjar. Grotesque flickering shadows loomed up on all sides as you progressed down the garden. Sometimes an owl hooted in the dark woods, or your blood would run cold at the call of a vixen for her mate. Nobody took their time down there at night; my imagination worked overtime when a stealthy wind rattled the door latch, and I sat fearful that a witch or wandering ghost might be queueing for our privvy. Then I'd take to my heels and scurry back to the safety of the house, my candle streaming flame and dripping grease in my flight from the dark and unknown terrors outside.

It was poor old Dad's job to empty the bucket at frequent intervals. He would dig a hole at the far end of the garden by day, and would then creep out under cover of darkness to do the dirty deed. He always bragged that his best crops grew down in that corner.

Down the Gyarden Path

Coust thee remember, old 'un, when we all had W.C.s
Away down in the gyarden, where we used to take our ease?
'Twere like a little palace, wi' zome mattin' on the floor;
Thic seat were scrubbed as white as snow – an' hung behind
   the door,
Upon a large an' sturdy nail, in pieces cut ta size,
All threaded on a length o' ztring, unheeding o' the flies,
Thee't vind a yup o' newspaper, its purpose plain ta zee.
In them days proper toilet rolls zeemed awful posh ta me.
Carbolic an' Jeyes Fluid zeemed ta ooze dru' every crack,
An' though we 'ad no chain ta pull, we never velt the lack.
A comp stuck in a jamjar were our only bit o' light,
An' it came in very 'andy when ole nature called at night.
Ta add ta the excitement, as thouse sat there in the dark,
A great fat hairy zpider on zome errand might embark.
'E'd zwing around quite gaily, clingin' to 'is zilken thread,
As, hypnotized, you watched an' prayed: 'Please, don't vall on
   me yud.'
Aye, many were the 'appy hours zpent there in reverie,
Gone, now, but not vorgotten – that ol' outzide W.C.

CHAPTER ELEVEN

Carnival Days

The focal point of our social life in Berry Hill was the YMCA building, known locally as the 'Ut and ably run by Mr and Mrs Milson 'Buller' Short. A lively committee would organize concerts and dances; whist drives, jumble sales and meetings for all kinds of groups and societies were regular features; and down some steps from the main hall, a billiard room helped many of the local men and youths while away the hours in a harmless and sociable way. The hut still stands today, though rather the worse for wear.

At the back there were, and still are, extensive sports grounds for rugby, soccer and tennis, not to mention a cricket pitch and pavilion and a well tended bowling green. In those days, too, the children's corner (now slightly neglected) was well equipped with swings, roundabouts, a six-seater hobby horse, a tall slide and a sandpit. When I was very small I tormented Mam to let me have a go on the slide – but when I at last climbed those steep iron steps and looked down at that narrow chute sweeping forever to the ground, I just flung back my head and howled. By this time the long queue of kids behind me was growing increasingly restive, and if Mam had not been around one of them would doubtless have given me a sharp shove. As it was, in the end everyone had to shuffle back down the steps to make way for her to rescue me. I never much fancied the slide after that.

There was a carnival procession every year, with floats and walking pageants, and its fun and colour attracted crowds from miles around. Berry Hill Silver Band strode out in front, and there was always a pretty carnival queen and her attendants to win admiration and loud applause from the hundreds lining the streets. A much favoured place from which to view the long, winding column of jazz bands, floats and fancy dress walkers was the pavement in front of S.J. Hawkins' grocery store at the crossroads between Christchurch, Berry Hill, Joyford and Five Acres. Another

Coleford Market Square the year Gladys Edey was crowned Carnival Queen.

A quiet day in Berry Hill – but the corner with S. J. Hawkins' store and the Globe pub was a favourite spot for watching the carnival procession.

of its attractions for some lay in the fact that it was just yards away from the popular Globe pub; for many of our menfolk, carnival day meant getting to the bar at opening time, knocking back beer or lethal scrumpy cider as if it were going out of fashion, and then stumbling from the door as soon as the band could be heard advancing to the crossroads. Standing there bleary-eyed, a pint still clutched in their hand and doubtless seeing a double procession passing them by, they would raise a few cheers, drop a couple of coppers in the collecting boxes – and then, as soon as the last float had disappeared round the corner, make a beeline back to the pub. There they would remain until the four-letter word 'Time!' was called by the weary but no doubt better-off landlord.

Meanwhile, the band would continue up Coverham, across the top, then down to the recreation ground, 'the Rec', via Zion Chapel Road. A local celebrity would help the queen hand out prizes to the lucky ones, after which everyone would rush to the various stalls and games scattered around the grounds. You could try your luck on the wheel of fortune, bowl for a pig on the sawdust-covered outside alley, throw some rings in hoopla, hope yours would be the lucky peg in the treasure hunt . . . Brightly decked trestle tables offered home-made sweets, cakes and toys, and for refreshment you could head for the cool tea marquee or the always well patronized beer tent. The band would play lively tunes at intervals throughout the afternoon, jazz bands strutted their stuff in the main arena and harassed committee members rushed around organizing the children's races. Not that all was feverish activity; at these annual events you often bumped into people you hadn't seen since the last carnival, so all over the grounds there were little knots of folk catching up on all the news and gossip.

To round off the day there would be a carnival dance in the hut, always fifty-fifty: half modern ballroom, half old-time. I was allowed to attend this great event when I was older, on the understanding that there would be some responsible adult around to take me home. I can never remember much bother from drunks or trouble-makers; at the first sign of any ill temper, a couple of burly committee members would show the offenders the door. A gang of Brylcreemed, pimply youths would be herded together at the far end of the room, close to the exit. We girls sat along one side of the floor, giggling together and pretending to ignore them. At the same time we'd be watching the older girls enviously, lost in admiration as, done up like film stars, they dipped and swooped with their partners to the latest quickstep or waltz.

When the M.C. announced the St Bernard waltz or veleta, that was our cue to grab another girl and join in the fun at last. As we all knew only the lady's steps, there would usually be a squabble over who should be the man; it was worst towards the end of the sequence, when a short waltz would inevitably see both partners moving in the same direction, tangling feet, falling over and irritating the serious dancers no end. There would then be nothing else to do but flee to the ladies' cloakroom and collapse in a tittering heap, after which we might or might not re-emerge to try our luck again. One way or another, we'd always be around for the

Alec's mother Lil Baldwin and friends with their Rumpelstiltskin pageant at Berry Hill Carnival.

last waltz and the perspiring band's rendition of 'God Save The King' that heralded the end of Berry Hill Carnival for another year.

Nearly every town and village in the Forest had an event of this kind; lots of them were fêtes much smaller than Berry Hill's festivities, but on our doorstep at Coleford was a carnival even bigger than ours. Always held on August Tuesday, it attracted competitors from all over, and you can be sure that we Berry Hillites didn't miss out on the fun. Several weeks before the big day, a contest would be held in Coleford Town Hall to select a carnival queen and her attendants. The judging was left to the audience, and the lucky few would be lined up and photographed for the weekly *Guardian* newspaper. One year, Gladys Edey of Coalway was a very popular winner, known to lots of the carnival crowd as an assistant at Pont and Adams' grocery and bakery store on the corner of St John's Street and Box Bush Road in town; the long procession of floats, walking tableaux and bands wound right past her place of work as it progressed through the town centre, up St John's Street and Staunton Road, and then along Victoria Road to the Buchanan Recreation Ground.

My cousin Alec Baldwin could always be relied upon to entertain the crowds with his weird and wonderful bikes and

Joyce's cousin Alec Baldwin's silly bikes were always a big draw at Coleford Carnival.

costumes. Every year he and his dad Joe came up with a mechanical miracle and an equally funny character, and they were often among the top prizes. On the Rec there was so much to see; I remember cossack dancers, clowns and motor cycle stuntmen as special attractions, but there would always be stilt walkers, fire eaters, a horticultural show – and in the evening, fireworks and floodlit dancing. To me, one of the most exciting parts of the day was trying to track down Dally Dock, the carnival mystery man. A misleading photograph of Dally would be published in the carnival programme, complete with false nose and glasses, and with a hat pulled well down over his forehead. The £2 prize – a reward well worth trying for – could be claimed only if the challenger carried a copy of the programme and was word-perfect with: 'You are Mr Dally Dock, the Coleford mystery man, and I claim the £2.' I never was successful, though on one occasion I realized, too late, that I had been standing right next to him in the crowd.

What great value Coleford Carnival was, at 1*s* in the stands and 6*d* to walk round. Perhaps too great value; rain or shine, the expensive attractions had to be paid for, and for all the committee's

The man with the money: everyone wanted to track down the mysterious Dally Dock at Coleford Carnival.

hard work, there was a spell when it had to be abandoned for several years. Although up and running again for a while, it has now been permanently abandoned. People no longer feel inclined to make fools of themselves to entertain others, and that's a fact of life that no amount of cajoling by local organizers will change. Yet there is so much emphasis placed these days on family fun — and what could epitomize the phrase more than a traditional community day out in which everybody can enjoy themselves?

CHAPTER TWELVE

Dance – and Romance

I got to know quite a few boys when I was a fourteen-year-old working in Turner's paper shop, serving them with their comics, sweets, stationery and so on. There would be friendly banter and good-natured teasing, and I would meet up with some of them on Saturday nights, when, after finishing work at six, I could be found in the queue for the second house of the pictures at Coleford. Four or five of my favourites went round in a gang, including one towards whom my feelings were rather more than friendly. The fact was, I was besotted with him. To me he was Mr Perfect from the top of his dark Brylcreemed curls, through his beautiful blue-grey eyes and long, curly lashes right down to his immaculate, highly polished shoes. He had only to walk through the shop door and my heart would go bump, my hands trembled and my knees turned to water. When I first knew him he worked in a gents' outfitters in Coleford. Somehow, I became a kind of honorary member of his gang, the only girl, and I liked the odds of five-to-one on. As I worked on the sweet counter, some of the old men would sometimes give me their sweet ration coupons, which meant that I nearly always had a few chocolates or toffees to share at the pictures. Looking back, I have an uneasy feeling that this might have been my main attraction. . . .

I was desperate to be near him, so much so that I started going to the Independent Chapel in Coleford, of which he was a member. I also struck up a friendship with one of his younger sisters, and by that means managed to worm my way into his home. His younger brother had been in my class at Bell's, though he had not been the same kind of dreamboat at all; he was always rushing off to play football somewhere, or returning with filthy knees and his shorts steeped in mud.

At last the day dawned when all my schemes paid off, and the blue-grey-eyed one asked me to go to the pictures with him in

Monmouth. I was on Cloud Nine, and took hours to get ready. I can't remember what was on; holding hands in the dark was all I needed, and when he gave me a quick goodnight kiss I was in heaven. We went out a few times after that, and might have continued to do so had he not been called up to do his National Service. I looked forward to his letters eagerly, and when at last they arrived I would read them over and over again. Love mingled with pride when his first leave came around, and I stepped out with him in his smart new uniform; it seemed as if all my dreams had come true.

Not for long, alas. I wanted to hear all about his new life in the army, and of how much he had missed me, but all he could talk about was some wretched girl called Rosemary. I curled up inside when he told me how beautiful she was, blonde and busty – unlike me. On and on he raved, and while I tried to keep a look of interest on my face, my poor heart was slowly breaking into little pieces. As we said goodnight, I shrugged away when he had the nerve to try to kiss me. Tears half blinded my eyes as I ran home down the lane, to the one place in the world I knew there was real love for me. In bed I pulled the blankets up over my head and cried and cried until I was almost sick. Broken heart? Shattered ego? Who's to say? We've all known it, and the hurting's just as bad, whatever we call it.

And of course, after a while, the pain began to ease. I talked myself into thinking I was well shot of him, and there were plenty more fish in the sea. I joined a Monday evening modern ballroom-dancing class at Coleford Town Hall, and it didn't matter much to me that I had already learned the rudiments from Auntie Vi; I wasn't there just for the dancing. Most of the young girls I hung around with were developing good figures, accentuated by tight sweaters. I was still as flat as a pancake, and was resigned to staying that way through life until my friend Barbara Greenaway came up with what I thought was a brilliant answer to my 'little' problem.

'If I was ta lend tha one o' my bras, o' butt, thee coust stuff some cotton wool in the cups. That'd do the trick.' I could hardly wait for the next Monday evening to come around, not least because I'd been longing to wear a lovely pale blue, wide-skirted dress someone had given me. It was fine from the waist down, but where there was no me at the top it hung loose and baggy in a most unprepossessing way. That night, I stood in front of the swing mirror and, pulling handfuls of cotton wool from a large roll, packed the bra as full as it would hold. When I slid the dress over my head and eased it down gently over my new bosoms, the result was beyond my wildest dreams. My voluptuous curves would have made film stars green with envy, and the dress could not have fitted better.

I grew more and more excited as I twirled and preened in front of the mirror, and discovered that I looked good from every angle. I couldn't wait to get to the Town Hall to knock 'em cold, and it was with some flair that I made my entry that night, flinging my coat over the back of my chair as I joined the girls. They looked me over in a puzzled kind of way, nudging each other slyly. But I pretended to take no notice, and rightly so, for before long I was having the time of my life, with partners galore. This happy state of affairs continued for quite a while as I waltzed, tangoed and foxtrotted the night away, wallowing in all the attention, and scornful of the girls consigned to shuffling round the floor with one another.

Of course none of this could last, and disaster struck while I was whirling round and round the floor to my favourite quickstep. My partner was quite tall, and as he held me in a vice-like grip, my bust was in close contact with his gyrating waist and my arms were stretched to the limit. It was at this point that I felt something creeping across the front of my dress, and, glancing down, discovered that what at the start of the evening had been proud and double and symmetrical was now single and distinctly lop-sided. Across the floor, a sinuous line of cotton wool blobs followed in my wake. There was nothing else to be done: I gave a strangled cry, disentangled myself from my hapless partner, grabbed my coat and hat and flew down the outside staircase into the night. My face was aflame with embarrassment and humiliation, and it was a long time before I dared show myself in the Town Hall again. My vanity had been my undoing, and though it's a trite and universal saying, I shall never forget Mam's very special way of warning me: 'Now doesn't thee vorget, our Joyce, as pride often comes avore a fall.'

CHAPTER THIRTEEN

V.E. Day

I was thirteen when the war on the home front ended with V.E. Day on 13 May 1945. I could not envisage a world without rationing, queues, restrictions, identity cards and gas masks; they had been a part of our everyday lives for so long, as much a part of the Forest to me as our wandering sheep. Indeed, we soon found out that, V.E. day or no, some of these irksome by-products of war would still be with us for years to come – but on that day in May it was simply a time for everyone to go wild with joy, festooning their houses and streets with dusty flags and tattered bunting that had last seen the light of day at George V's silver jubilee and his son George VI's coronation not long after that. Bonfires were thrown together quickly on top of the highest hills, and by pooling resources most neighbourhoods managed to rustle up some kind of tea for the children and pensioners. Bells that had been kept silent except to sound a warning of imminent invasion now had the joyous task of ringing out in celebration of victory, and the pubs did nearly as well as the churches and chapels with their thanksgiving services.

Auntie Doris and her little Graham came round to our house; by this time, Vi and Eric and their two children had moved to Andover, and we missed them very much. Even Mam took a taste of the bottle of my stepfather Bill's home-made wine that had been brought over by Doris, and like Dad, she was on her best form for years. We were all just so grateful that the agony was nearly over – 'nearly', because the spectre of Japan still hovered in the background; but that was all a long way off, and nothing was going to be allowed to spoil this wonderful day.

Barbara Greenaway came down to ask Mam if I could go with her to the Bicknor dance that night – and to my astonishment she said yes; I felt Bill's wine had played some part in this decision. Riding my luck, I persuaded her to press one of my fairly decent

V.E. Day celebrations in Gloucester Road, Coleford.

Sunday best dresses, and after polishing my black lace-up school shoes, I decided this would be a good time to make use of a pair of rayon stockings sent me as a present by Auntie Vi. These had to be held up on my skinny legs with garters made from knicker elastic, but I felt like Betty Grable in the first pair of see-through stockings I had ever worn. Looking back, now, I realize the then unknown Nora Batty would have been nearer the mark.

As usual on such high days, I was nearly sick with excitement long before it was time to call for Barbara, who added to the glamour of the night by lending me some lipstick to apply as best I might. This was really living! The Bristol Blue bus we caught at the top of the lane was crammed with people, singing and shouting, but there was enough room for us by the time they had shuffled down the saloon. The conductor, entering fully into the spirit of the hour, seemed none too worried about collecting fares.

The dance hall was equally heaving. I wish I could remember more: the tunes, the band, the partners; I just recall the wonderful electric atmosphere in that little golden oasis in the dark of the English countryside that night, our joy and relief overwhelming any concern about crushed ribs, trampled toes, smoke-filled lungs. Barbara and I had long been separated by the crowd, but now and again I caught a glimpse of her blonde mane as she was whirled around the floor. There was never a shortage of partners when she was around, and I could only sit on the sidelines admiring – with no rancour, on this night, at least – my pretty friend's vivacity and allure. When the band eventually ran out of steam, and all the howls of protest in the world could not stem the inevitability of the last waltz and the national anthem, I looked for her among the happy revellers; but she was nowhere to be seen, and when I went back to the cloakroom to seek her out one last time, the attendant told me she had been gone some time.

With a sinking heart, I realized I would have to make my own way home. It was past 1 p.m., V.E. Day no more, and the moon was flitting in and out of the clouds, bright enough one minute, the next as black, as they used to say, as your father's hat. I started off up the long road, holding tight to my purse, my footsteps echoing unnervingly. Tree branches hung down whispering together, and rustling eerily in a sudden breeze, as I crept up the steep Chapel Hill. From time to time the figures of large strangers would lurch out of the darkness, unstable from having celebrated too well. My black lace-ups pinched my toes as I shuffled along close to the hedgerows, trying to melt with the shadows as I heard yet more footsteps down the long, winding road. There was nothing left by now of my earlier euphoria; I was just a very scared little girl longing for the safety of her home and her bed.

The worst part of the walk home was having to pass Christchurch burial ground. Here I took to my heels and ran as fast as my aching feet would allow, resisting the morbid temptation to see whether the spirits had had a V.E. Day celebration of their own. Up to Christchurch Cross and down the red ash path to Marian's Lane I ran, not daring to look back or to left or right. Even when I had reached our front gate my over-active imagination still half-expected a cold, clammy hand to reach out and tap me on the shoulder.

In those days nobody bothered to lock their doors, so I was able to creep quietly to my bedroom unheard; Mam was not waiting up for me, for once, no doubt worn out by the day's excitements. I didn't need much rocking, and on the following day I was able to sleep in. I never did tell Mam of that nightmarish walk home; she presumed that Barbara and I had returned home with the rest of the Berry Hill gang, and I said nothing to suggest otherwise. I didn't want her to worry. And besides, I was crafty enough to realize that if she had learned the truth, there would have been no more late dances for me.

CHAPTER FOURTEEN

The Homecoming

The lifting of blackout restrictions was one of the first steps towards the normality of peace-time, though we did not feel its full impact until the shorter days returned later in the year. Other than that, life in the Forest went on much as usual: long queues, most goods in short supply, no end to rationing in sight. Pessimists talked of the war in Japan dragging on and on, and it was against this background that the quantum leap was made to end hostilities by devastating Hiroshima and Nagasaki with atom bombs. Few at that time – few lay people, at least – foresaw the long-term consequences of that course of action. We were simply thankful to see the end of a devastating, soul-destroying era we had at times thought would last forever.

So V.J. Day rolled around, a day of celebration chosen more arbitrarily than the spontaneous outburst of joy on 13 May. And for other reasons, too, the occasion did not have the same lustre for our family, for we were trying to come to terms with a shattering tragedy of our own. Auntie Doris, one of my natural mother's sisters, had been working shifts at a factory called Pine End in Lydney, where trees were processed into plywood. Her husband was dead and her young son Graham was living with his father's sisters at the top of Ready Penny Pitch, between Hillersland and Christchurch, in order to give Doris the chance to earn a living to support the little fellow. This gave her a degree of independence out of the ordinary in our tight-knit family – so much so that it was a few days before we suddenly realized that we had not seen or heard from her for a while. When she was eventually discovered, she had been lying dead at the bottom of her stairs for three days. She was a hard-working soul with a weak heart and a lame leg, and the strain of the factory, cleaning her house and tending her big garden had been too much for her. What made it harder was the thought of all those years of drudgery, doing all she could for the

Three sisters: Elsie, Joyce's real mother; seated, the tragic Doris; and right, Vi.

war effort, only for her to be taken from us before she could enjoy the fruits of the final victory. Poor Mam's heart was broken, and she was never the same again. As for me, it was my first encounter with death, my first taste of its devastating finality.

I was at a loss to know how to comfort Mam, her profound grief making all my efforts to cheer her sound hollow and futile. Only when news of her son Bill's impending demob arrived did she perk up a little – but this was the aftermath of war, and even the happy endings were not all that they might have been. She had waved farewell to a fresh-faced youth who was little more than a child. The battle-wearied figure who returned was a serious, grave-faced stranger, and Mam and Dad were shocked by the change in him. Still, when he marched up our path, they tried to act as though the years apart had counted for nothing. He brought us all presents, souvenirs he had picked up on his travels, and mine were a pretty necklace of gold and silver coloured leaves and a beautiful little clock with flowers on its face and a silver stand, both of them from Rome.

But Bill's thoughts were elsewhere – with Peggy, his fiancée for several years, whom he had met while stationed in Wales. No sooner had he done the rounds of friends and relatives in our area and he was off, looking very smart in his demob suit and laden with presents for his girl and her family. He would be with them for a couple of weeks, he told us, during which time they would arrange a date for the wedding. He had kept all her letters and brought them home in a small suitcase, obviously very proud of them; she had written every week all the time he had been away, he said.

He was not gone long – two days, to be exact – and when he returned he was a broken man. He told us that when he arrived at Peggy's door he was let in by her mother, who was wearing the engagement ring he had given the girl. It was then that she broke the news that his sweetheart had married somebody else more than a year previously, but had continued writing to him as if nothing were amiss. At the time, as a young teenager, and having seen the effect her deceit had had on the man I regarded as my big brother, I felt I could cheerfully have murdered Peggy. It still seems extraordinary behaviour to me today, even given the extraordinary nature of the times. The immediate consequence was that Bill went on the drink. Night after night he would crawl home out of his mind, but Mam would never put up a word of protest. She realized he was trying to forget, to cope with his grief and pain; but we felt helpless to comfort him and could only look on as his personality changed from that of a cheery extrovert to a bitter, lonely man. He never trusted a woman again, and when, at happy times, the odd flash of his old self shone through, it only served to emphasize what he and we had lost.

It was the time that Carter's factory was being built at the top of High Nash, a little way out of Coleford, and Bill was successful in finding work with Prodrite, one of the contractors. He got on so well with them that they took him on permanently in a job that involved his travelling around the country from site to site. This suited him. The war and its aftermath had left him rootless and restless and besides, there was a dire shortage of space for him in our little bungalow. To sleep at night he had to cram his six-foot-two frame on to our little sofa, and there was always Dad's terrible

Uncle Bill in the uniform of the Welsh Guards. He returned from war a changed man.

cough to ensure that he did not get much rest. Perhaps it was not surprising that, to Mam's bitter disappointment, he was soon on his travels again. In the final analysis he survived her by just seven months, dying a lonely bachelor at the age of fifty-six.

CHAPTER FIFTEEN

Friends and Neighbours

Though we were ceasing to be children, my best friend Joyce and I still went for long walks in the beautiful woods surrounding our homes, each season in its turn bringing familiar but ever-fresh magic. Spring was always a miracle, the forest returning to life, teeming with tiny buds and shoots which would soon turn into canopies and carpets to delight the eye. We knew where the dewy white and mauve violets flourished on a high bank, and kept watch on the hawthorn bushes until they sprouted their first covering of leaves, which we children called 'bread and cheese', and found quite edible. We loved to go looking for birds' nests down lanes where blackbirds, robins, blue-tits and thrushes had been building their snug little homes, and it was always a thrill to discover a clutch of blue eggs speckled with red, taking great care not to disturb the nest for fear of the mother blackbird deserting it. Sometimes we would be lucky enough to discover a wren's cleverly designed little home, safe from predators deep in a mossy bank.

After a while the 'skinnies' would emerge, gaping mouths ever-ready to be filled with insects, small worms and other appetizing fare by their tireless parents. We were always heart-broken if we came across a nest in which the eggs had become cold, or stumbled on the naked, pitiful little body of a chick that had somehow fallen from its safe haven.

Fragile white and mauve anemones sprang up under the beech and larch, celandines gleamed and winked among the young grass, and later a smudge of blue proclaimed the presence of bluebells, welcome invaders of our woods that spread their subtle scent through every glade. We enjoyed many a picnic beside the Wye in the deep gorge below Symonds Yat Rock, and there was a rickety old bridge used by workmen over which we'd pass, never daring to look down at the cold, deep, dangerous waters gliding beneath us.

I frequently took shorter walks nearer home, accompanied by our little fox terrier Peggy, the main purpose being to gather firewood for our ever-hungry kitchen grate. I always carried a stout piece of string to secure my booty; there's an art to all things, even tying up and carrying firewood, and I had learned it at an early age from my Mam and Dad.

Sometimes I would meet our nearest neighbour, Mr Cooper, tapping the ground in front of him with his stick, in search of obstacles. His blindness did not deter him from his daily walk, and I always saw his finding his way around as little short of miraculous. On rare occasions he might wander too far from his usual beat, and his daughter Aliph Roberts, who lived in an adjoining cottage, would be forced to raise the alarm. There would then be a search of the woods by his son-in-law John, his grandson Arthur and assorted neighbours, while Aliph kept anxious vigil by the back stile. He was always found eventually, safe and sound and ready for his supper; and being a stubborn old Forester he would be all set for his travels again the next morning, much to his daughter's dismay.

My friend Barbara Greenaway, with blonde hair, blue eyes and dimples inherited from her mother, lived near the top of our lane.

Barbara Greenaway, who died tragically young.

The disaster of the V.E. Day dance was a reminder that she was a couple of years older than me, and far more outgoing. She had four brothers, Ken, Keith, Tony and Norman, and their father was an expert carpenter who was kept busy every Christmas during the war years making dolls' houses, scooters, mini-wheelbarrows and so on for children of local families. Almost opposite them lived the Teagues – a grand old Gloucestershire name – or more specifically old Mrs Teague, her son Harold, his wife Ruby and their baby daughter Shirley. She was a pretty wee thing with a mop of curls, and it's hard not to believe that they named her after my favourite film star of the time, the phenomenal little Miss Temple.

I often took her for a ride in her pram, or helped her gran to baby-sit on the odd occcasion when Harold and Ruby were out for a couple of hours. Sometimes when she was tired she would start crying, and to cheer her up I'd do a silly dance, flinging my arms and legs around and pulling funny faces. It didn't always impress Shirley, but it would usually tickle old Mrs Teague, if nothing else. If all else failed, I would treat the little tot to some of my off-key singing, at which she would sensibly nod off in self defence. Harold owned and worked a small coal level some way down in the wood – until, one sad day, he never returned home. A sudden rock fall turned his happy-go-lucky wife into a heartbroken young widow; life was cheaper in the Forest in those days.

Next to the Teagues lived the Symonds: miner Ted, his wife and their lads Frank, Jimmy and baby Royston; there was certainly no shortage of boys in our corner of Dean. Ted was one of those chaps known for his dry wit, a characteristic of the Forest; and my Dad aside, he had the broadest 'Vurest' accent I've ever heard. Opposite them lived Ivy Jones, her son Michael and her brother Reg, who mended shoes from a small shed in their garden. He was never short of customers and he did especially well during the war years. People saved not just money but precious clothing coupons by keeping their footwear in good repair, rather than splashing out on new. I was always happy to visit him, sniff the all-pervading smell of new leather that filled his workshop and watch with amusement while a machine of his with a row of round brushes whirred and hummed. Not that Reg got much custom from Dad, who would always try to cobble his boots at home, using any good pieces from discarded pairs in order to keep out the wet.

All these folks were good friends, as well as neighbours. So were others like the Wilsons, with their children Jack and Kath, who lived next to a green tump opposite the King's Head. In fact, over a wide area of Berry Hill, Five Acres, Hillersland, Short Standing, Joyford, the Lonk and Christchurch, we were really a tight-knit community in which almost everybody knew everybody else. Most family histories were more or less common knowledge, including their wealth or lack of it, their characteristics, and any skeletons rattling around in their cupboards. If anyone was misguided enough to put on airs and graces, the usual expression trotted out was: 'Uh, 'er mam used ta chew bread vur ower ducks.' When I was small I took this refined insult quite literally, and concluded it was a dreadful way to make a living.

You could say Foresters have always had an almost tribal instinct. If a gang of youths from Broadwell or Coleford, each about a mile away, ever descended on Berry Hillers' territory, it would always be the signal for a good old set-to, with fists flying along with sticks and stones. But if Coleford or Broadwell were ever visited by raiders from Lydney or Cinderford, then old enmities would be forgotten in defence of the common area. With this background, the problems of true outsiders, or 'Vurriners', trying to settle in the area can be easily imagined. At first they would be viewed with suspicion, with their behaviour scrutinized carefully for any sign of 'uppitiness' or decadence. But if they were in any kind of unavoidable difficulty, such as illness or bereavement, then they quickly felt the comforting touch of helping hands stretching out at them from all directions. Today, you will find almost as many Vurriners as true Foresters living in the Dean; but scratch a little way beneath the surface of most natives and that warm-hearted, generous nature is still there, responding to genuine need just as quickly as it did in days gone by.

Secret Places

I know of secret places where the willows bend,
And little whispering streams play hide-and-seek;
Where minnows dart
And dragonflies swoop from the sky.
But no-one else knows — only I.

I know of secret places where the bluebells sway,
And timid deer hide deep within the shade;
Where thrushes sing
And honeysuckle climbs up high.
But no-one else knows — only I.

I know of secret places where the plaintive sea
Beats on the wind-lashed rocks, then runs away;
Where seagulls scream
And long-haired mermaids sigh.
But no-one else knows — only I.

I know of secret places where, when darkness falls,
The phantom owl glides softly through the glade;
Where moonbeams dance
And black-robed witches fly.
But no-one else knows — only I.

CHAPTER SIXTEEN

Williams and Cotton

I had been working in the paper shop about eighteen months when I was offered the chance of another job. On the opposite side of the road from us was a busy branch of the Williams and Cotton chain of grocery stores, which had shops in many parts of the Forest, and they were always regarded as good employers. At that time the manager was Perce Powell, but I was better acquainted with the cashier, Myrtle Morgan, who was a regular customer of ours and usually had a smile or a few words for me. One day, when my workmates Betty and Dorothy were out the back having their morning break, Myrtle slipped in and asked whether I might be interested in a vacancy across the road; if so, I should pop over and have a word with the manager as soon as I could.

I found time to nip across during my dinner hour. Perce Powell had apparently been keeping his eye on me, too, and said he had been impressed by the way I gave change and got on with the customers generally. If I joined him, my hours would be from 8.30 a.m. to 6 p.m. Monday to Saturday, half day Thursday, and my wages would be £1 7s 6d a week. It didn't take much thinking about. The pay, incredibly, was three times as much as I had been earning at the paper shop, and there was the added incentive of no more getting up for morning delivery rounds. Agreeing with Mr Powell to hand in a week's notice at the Red and White was a great deal easier than confronting Mr Turner to do the deed, but I plucked up my courage and confronted him. He was not a happy man. He even visited me at home one evening in an attempt to make me change my mind, and offered a rise to £1 5s. It was not easy to find honest employees, he explained. None of any of this cut much ice with me. I couldn't help thinking that if I was worth that kind of money now, why couldn't he have offered it me before? So it was I said goodbye to the Red and White and took on my new role as a grocery assistant at Williams and Cotton.

I found all my new colleagues very kind and helpful, and Myrtle Morgan – 'Miss', in shop hours – took me under her wing. We have been friends ever since. I was fitted with a starched white overall, though in truth I was so small that it was quite hard to find one my size. In fact Auntie Vi was roped in to take up the hem a couple of inches and put a tuck in the long sleeves, as Mam had never been very handy with needle and thread. The buttons were made of bone, and could be removed before the garment was given to the laundry man at the end of the week.

One side of the shop had a wide, polished wood counter running the length of it, while on the other side was the marble-topped 'fats' counter, for butter, lard, margarine, cheese and bacon. At the foot of the stairs leading to the first floor was the open-topped cashier's office where 'Miss' reigned supreme. Any bills or requests for change were dealt with through a small pigeon-hole set in the front, between high sheets of patterned frosted glass. Flanking the other side of the office, an old counter adorned by large brass scales was used to weigh and pack many of the goods sold in the shop.

We had our own brand of tea, sold in thick paper packets bearing our name and a blue and white design. Sugar was weighed up into blue bags of differing weights, two pounds, a pound and halves, and since hardly anything came ready packaged in those days, we were constantly on the go making up packets of biscuits, lentils, rice, dried fruit – when we could get it in the war years – dried peas, maize, sago, tapioca and even soap flakes, which would make you sneeze forever and ever if you got them up your nose.

At the back of the shop, out of sight of the customers, sides of bacon had to be boned ready to be put through the slicer, and this was men's work. The flitches arrived covered in muslin cloths, which were useful as dishrags or dusters after they had been boiled and bleached. There was no refrigeration, and I shall never forget the first time I saw a side of bacon being boned on a very hot summer's day. As each bone was being cut out, I could see a mass of wriggling maggots beneath the skin. The men would gouge these out with their sharp boning knives, after which the meat would be swabbed down with vinegar and water, and then wiped dry. It made my poor stomach heave, and I went off bacon for quite

Newland Street, Coleford, in the late 1920s. Williams and Cotton's shop is fourth from the left.

a while after that, but nobody who continued to eat it that warm summer seemed any the worse for it. What a sign of changing times, though, for this was a successful chain of shops that was known far and wide for its high standards and hygiene.

Women were never allowed to handle bacon in those days. It was firmly believed that if a woman touched meat at her wrong time of the month, the whole side would turn rotten. It is astonishing to think of such taboos surviving well into living memory, but that particular rule was widely applied throughout the grocery trade. Huge cheeses had to be skinned in readiness to be cut into pieces that in turn would be sliced into family-sized portions by wire. During the war and indeed throughout the rationing period, manual workers including miners, farmers, building labourers and the like were allowed an extra weekly allowance of cheese; the standard ration was scarcely enough to bait a mousetrap.

Would we put up with rationing if, God forbid, it were ever forced on us again? I suppose we would. In recent times, the

Falklands War was a reminder that we are a patriotic race, if our backs are up against the wall. Nevertheless, what a dire time it all was. I can even recall, still, the number I was given at the outbreak of war and retained until the withdrawal of rationing in the early 1950s – ODZH/75/3. My ration book was blue, Mam and Dad's were fawn, and contained in their pages were sheets of 'points' of varying values, to be used for cereals, tinned goods, dried eggs and such commodities. Another page carried tea and soap coupons, and there were even bread units, later, though they were never used to my knowledge. One page was reserved for fats, our cheese and bacon rations. We were allowed two ounces of butter, four of lard, two of cheese, four of the horrid Special Margarine, eight of sugar, four of bacon, two of tea, a solitary egg and three pints of milk. Members of the forces home on leave were issued with an emergency coupon for the week, which could be taken to any shop of their choice.

As can be imagined, there was a lot of bureaucracy attached to all of this, and woe betide you if you were unfortunate enough to lose or accidentally destroy your precious ration book. You had to apply to the Food Office for a new one, which involved filling in mountains of forms in triplicate. By the same token, we shop assistants had to keep on top of the paperwork. All the coupons had to be cut out as they were spent, and put away carefully in a drawer; it was then someone's job, at the end of the week, to add up the totals and report them to the Food Office. An added complication was the fact that not many people paid for their groceries as they carried them out of the store. It would be: 'Put it on me bill, o' butty', and off they'd trot. It was all cash when they did come up with the payment, needless to say. There were no cheques, since for most of us banks were strictly for the toffs. The under manager, Gordon Roberts, would set off on his bike, a different round each day, to call on customers to take their orders and receive anything owed on the previous week's bill. The orders would be given to a counter assistant to make up, with each item placed in line on the provisions side and checked by another assistant before being packed tidily into a cardboard box. Delivery by van was the responsibility of Sid Powell, Perce's brother, and he would see to it that the bill would be tucked down among the tins and bottles, and that the customer's name and address were writ large across some readily visible sugar bag or cheese wrapper.

The weekly delivery of tobacco and cigarettes had to be smuggled through the shop, up the stairs and into Perce's little office on the first floor. The precious cargo was then shared out as fairly as possible among a long list of our regular nicotine-addicted customers. Each small pile was wrapped carefully in cheese paper, on which was written the customer's name and the price of the contents. This ritual was carried on until supplies flowed freely once again, and cigarettes went back on display for sale to all.

From all of this you might have gathered that I enjoyed every bit of shop work. One of my specialities, it turned out, was dealing with notoriously bad-tempered or difficult customers. I looked upon it as a personal challenge to make them at least smile, and if there was a chuckle, too, that was a bonus. I soon learned who had to be handled with kid gloves, and those with whom I could share some traditional Forest banter. My secret ambition was always to work on the fats counter. I longed to be cutting out blocks of lard, butter and margarine to weigh and wrap into tidy little packages, and I watched enviously as Doris Kear or Marie Bowley expertly wielded the wire to slice cheese into neat wedges. Marie's elder sister Kath worked on my side of the shop, and some evenings all the staff would descend on their house after work for a game of cards. Our Bill had taught me quite a few games and I enjoyed those evenings, at which Mrs Bowley always made sure we had a cup of tea and some home-made cakes between games and the girls' brother Gordon was another friendly face. Sometimes I was lucky enough to pick up the kitty of 'yuppenies' at the end of the session, and I'd waltz off home as if I'd won the pools.

The Powell brothers were a pretty ill-matched pair, always at loggerheads. Even their politics were poles apart, manager Perce siding with the Tories and delivery man Sid a dyed-in-the-wool Socialist, like so many Forest people with working-class roots. One evening Sid came struggling through the shop with a tea chest brimming over with rubbish to be taken to one of the open tips for disposal. I had just swept the place through, and was sprinkling sawdust over the wooden boards when some remark of Perce's so upset Sid that he promptly tipped the contents of the chest all over the floor. We all leapt away as rotten tomatoes, bacon bones, cheese skins and much else besides shot out in all directions. The atmosphere was electric as he stormed out, slamming the door behind him, and everyone set about clearing up the mess as Perce muttered something not at all brotherly. There must have been a few of us dying to burst out into fits of giggles, but one look at the managerial face convinced us that this was neither the time nor the place.

I loved my time at Williams and Cotton, and it was great to be able to give Mam a whole pound each week and still have seven and six all to myself. By this time, however, a few of my friends were working at Pine End, the plywood factory some five miles from Coleford, at Lydney, where my tragic Auntie Doris worked until her death. They bragged of the big money to be earned on shifts there, every weekend off, paid holidays and I don't know what else. Nobody mentioned, before it was too late, the sheer soul-destroying monotony, the boring repetition, the unsociable hours. My head was quite swimming with thoughts of giving Mam two pounds a week and still having enough to buy new clothes whenever I felt like it; it seemed an easy step to give up my shop life and become a factory hand.

Service with a Smile

Hypermarkets, supermarkets, serve your blinkin' selves,
Push your trolley round and round and grab things off the
   shelves.
Struggle through the milling crowds who clutter up the aisles,
Try to find a cashout – you could wander round for miles.
Join on to the shortest queue, by now you feel a wreck,
The customer in front of you will always pay by cheque.
Then after you have waited for eternity, it seems,
When finally you reach your goal, it's then the cashier
   screams:

'You'd better use the other till, I'm going for my break.'
And as she slams the cashout drawer, you groan: 'For goodness'
  sake,
Can't you just do this lot for me?' She shrugs, then flits away.
So you must join another queue — and all this just to pay!

It makes me feel nostalgic for those good old days of yore,
When everyone was welcome at our little grocer's store.
We'd stand behind the counter in our overalls of white,
A smile for every customer, for they were always right.
'Good morning, Mr. Brown, oh, yes, we ordered you that cheese,
As soon as it arrives we'll pop it round' — we aimed to please.
'And how's your mother keeping now? I hear she's been quite
  ill.
Right, half a pound of sausages, I'll put them on the bill.'
The manager would hover near, to keep us on our toes.
Our modern shops will never match the service found in those.
So 'serve yourself' is progress? Well, I guess it's here to
  stay.
But I for one would much prefer the stores of yesterday.

CHAPTER SEVENTEEN

Whistle While You Work

The Pine End factory was a shock to the system. On the early morning shift I had to be up and waiting for the works bus at Christchurch Cross by 4.30 a.m., and even in my early teens that spooky old churchyard had my imagination working overtime. I was usually the only passenger to be picked up at that stop, and I was always thankful to see the bus headlights coming into view.

That first morning I arrived at Pine End I was jostled along by a crowd lacking only Gracie Fields striding along at its head singing 'Sing As You Go'. How much we've lost since those days of full employment when Britain relied on its manufacturing industries, and its manufacturing industries relied on its labour force. After clocking in, I was overwhelmed by the stench of glue and ammonia, not to mention the cigarette fumes of Woodbine and Craven A – the one the advertisements told us 'will not affect your throat' – as the smokers among us took their last drags in the toilets and cloakroom. Nearly all the women wore headscarves as turbans, both to shield their hair from the clouds of dust and to disguise headsful of Dinkie curlers. I was lucky enough not to need these harsh little torturers, since the rage for short hair had seen my previously flowing auburn locks spring into curls. This saved me time and money, since all it needed was a quick brush and comb, and I had no use for perms.

Out on the factory floor I thought my eardrums would burst at the sound of the machines clanking and whirring. A charge hand led me to where a small gang of women was already busy transferring large, thin sheets of plywood from a glue edging machine on to a pallet on the floor. This operation had to be done with great care; otherwise, the whole piece tore apart, for the glue needed time to harden. By and large, the job was simple enough, and even I soon got the hang of it. There was one time, though, when things did not go as smoothly as usual. My mate Edith Thomas and I were working on opposite sides of the pallet. I was miles away, and she must have been, too, for one minute we were doing our loading job and the next we were buried under a pile of fragmented plywood. The foreman was not at all amused, but what made the incident live forever in our memories was the song being played over the tannoy on the Light Programme's *Music While You Work* as we sheepishly tidied up the mess: 'Why Should I Weep, Why Should I Sigh?'

I looked forward to that programme. Most of the girls sang along to the music, but as I had the world's worst singing voice, I'd whistle instead. I was forever whistling, and I'd only do so louder when older people, including Mam and Dad, wagged their fingers at me and quoted that old adage:

> *A whistling woman and a crowing hen*
> *Are neither good to God or men.*

I often found myself sitting next to Stan Phipps on the works' bus. He and his family were very well respected, and he in particular was known for his fine voice and piano playing. I knew him as the father of two of my old Christchurch schoolmates, Myrtle and Valerie, and found him a friendly figure, quite short with a mop of curly hair and wickedly sparkling eyes. One morning, I suggested it might be a good idea to liven the bus up with a song or two, and he grinned in approval. 'Cous't thee sing, then, o' butty?' he asked. 'No, I con't, but I con whistle a bit,' I replied. Most mornings after that, our sleepy, irritable workmates would be treated to spirited renditions of songs old and new. Sad to say, our efforts attracted only abuse and scowls from an audience more intent on catching a last nap – but Stan and I, being of that annoying breed that's always bright and bubbly in the morning, enjoyed our duets so much that we carried on regardless.

Whistling was also my subconscious defence against the dark. Whether picking my way down the lane at the end of an evening shift or waiting for the bus beside that eerie graveyard, I would fill the air around me with the reassuring strains of 'Twelfth Street Rag', 'Stardust' or whatever tune was on my mind. Our nearest neighbour up the lane, Mrs Roberts, once amazed me by saying that she could set the clock by my whistling. I hadn't realized it could penetrate stone walls.

Although the money was good at Pine End, and I had good friends there in Vi and Myrtle Davies and others, I never really took to the work. I missed the shop customers, and having to use my tiny brain a bit. What I did enjoy were the harmless pranks and good-natured teasing of the factory. I remember Auntie Vi giving me one of her frocks for work. It was bright yellow with a white pattern on it, and I thought it looked quite smart, especially with my auburn hair. I went to work feeling quite glamorous, but inevitably, not for long. 'Thic dress do make tha look just like a' egg yolk, o' butt,' some bright spark called out. There was no answer to that, other than never wearing that dress to the factory again.

By that time I was getting a lot of pain from a grumbling appendix, and Dr Tandy decided that it would be better out than in. It wasn't long before a brown envelope dropped through the letterbox, and I was summoned to Lydney Hospital for my operation. I took the letter along to the personnel office at Pine End, and they were nice and told me my job would be there for me when I was well again. I thanked them for that, but deep down I knew that my factory days had come to an end.

CHAPTER EIGHTEEN

Under the Knife

Now here's a funny thing, as Max Miller used to say. By a strange coincidence, my Auntie Vi's husband Eric parted company with his appendix at Lydney Hospital on the same day that I lost mine. Neither of us had ever been in hospital before, and while I had been quite looking forward to a new experience, poor Eric was scared stiff. I remember overhearing two young nurses giggling together about this chap who had just been admitted to the men's ward. It seemed that he had tried desperately to persuade them that it was all a big mistake. He swore that there was nothing wrong with him, and could he please go home? I decided not to let on about our relationship, in the hope of picking up more tasty gossip with which to regale Auntie Vi and tease her hubby when life returned to normal.

It was all very strange that first night, and for a long time I lay awake, listening to the snores and coughs of other patients. White-shaded electric lights were pulled down almost to the floor, and a nurse sat quietly at a desk at the top end of the room. Eventually I drifted off to sleep, not without some pangs of home-sickness.

The next I knew, all hell was breaking loose around me – scurrying feet, swishing curtains, a firm hand on my shoulder, a cheery 'Wakey, wakey', just to prove it wasn't some horrible dream. I opened one eye, and stared in disbelief at the big clock on the wall: 5.30 a.m. I opened the other eye, and the clock did not change its mind. 5.30! Why do hospitals do this? There was no time for such philosophical questions then, however, since it was clear that I was on the helter-skelter ride to the operating theatre. First it was a cup of tea, while the other patients tucked in to what suddenly seemed perfectly good and decent hospital fare of porridge and bacon and eggs. Then, more horrible by far, was my first experience of an enema, followed by a hot bath after it had done its work. This was a nasty shock, but worse was to come. I had hardly settled back in my bed when a trolley full of surgical mysteries was wheeled by my side. I was puzzled to see the nurse pick up a shaving brush and a mug of hot water – and felt I was going to die of embarrassment when she told me the reason why. She told me of the reaction of this funny chap she'd just dealt with on the men's ward. 'But I've had a shave this morning,' he'd insisted indignantly. It was another little gem to add to the dossier of Eric stories, but I confess I was in no condition to feel more than slightly cheered by it at the time.

The nurse's final act at my bedside was to paint my stomach a pretty shade of pink, after which it was time for the backless gown, the white cap and thick white woollen socks. An injection dried my saliva and left me with a raging thirst, and I lay like this for what seemed an age before I was lifted on to a trolley and wheeled to the theatre. My last memory of life with an appendix was of being given an injection and told to count to ten. The next I knew, the ward clock that had told me it was 5.30 a.m. had ticked on ten hours to 3.30 p.m., and my thirst was as strong as ever. Mam and Vi were vague figures at my bedside that evening – and I discovered that it really did hurt when I laughed, or coughed. The next morning life was much more like normal. That first cup of tea and breakfast in bed were heaven, and as I was the youngest on the ward, several of the other patients spoiled me with gifts of fruit and sweets from their lockers.

Mam and Vi clubbed together to hire a taxi from Charlie Collett's garage at Christchurch, a car equally in demand for weddings and funerals. I felt like a queen stepping into it that day, though I was still walking gingerly, afraid of jarring my side. Eric hobbled into the front seat beside the driver, Simon Thomas. He had become very blasé about hospitals by this time, tossing the odd medical phrase into the conversation and bragging about how the op had never given him a moment's worry. Of course Vi, Mam and I were all in on the true story, so allowed ourselves a secret smile; but it was still Eric who had the last laugh on me.

Dear old Mam had made sure to take all my clean clothes to the hospital for my homecoming – everything, that is, except a pair of knickers. Nobody would have been any the wiser, of course –

except for the fact that blabbermouth Vi just couldn't resist imparting this highly personal and embarrassing information to the two sniggering males in the front. I could cheerfully have wrung her neck – and the feeling didn't go away, as Simon Thomas teased me about it for years.

CHAPTER NINETEEN

'Doughnuts!'

It was several weeks after my operation before Dr Tandy was satisfied that I was fit to work again, and as Pine End had lost its appeal, I was happy when I was offered a job in the bakery of Birts Stores, just across the road from my old employers Williams and Cotton. In fact Williams and Cotton, big players in the Forest grocery game, had bought Birts a few years earlier, but were still happy to trade under the old identity. The pound notes that rolled in were just the same, whatever the name over the window.

Birts was a large grocery store with a separate cake shop to the front and a bakery tucked away on the Dram Road at the back; you could also get to it through a passageway running between the store and the cake shop. My new boss was Harry Whincup, a First World War veteran who was wounded in the leg as a cavalry officer. He was a striking enough figure, with a mop of white hair, beetling eyebrows, brown eyes and a long face; and although most who came across him would put him down as one of those 'strict but fair' bosses that were so prevalent at that time, when I got to know him better I realized that he had a puckish sense of humour.

An older man, also an old warrior, was Mr Conduit, who came in for a few hours most days to help out. He had lived in the Forest for donkeys' years, running a smallholding with his wife at the bottom of Whitecliff, off the road down to Newland and Clearwell; but he originated from Wolverhampton, and when he talked you would never have believed that he had left the Black Country. He must have been about seventy, with a slight stoop, grey hair, blue eyes and even bushier brows than his boss Mr Whincup. Some of us thought he was a bit slow on the uptake, sometimes, but he was a dear old chap and an assiduous worker, too.

My other colleague was Kath Davies, who had been in the forces in the Second World War. We soon became friends, and remain so to this day. It was left to her to show me the ropes, and at the same time she set me a good example with her proficiency and capacity for hard work. I started by cleaning out the big, heavy mixing bowls, which were in constant use making doughs and cake mixtures. Then there were the wide bun trays to grease, ready for the next batch of lardies, Chelsea buns, Eccles cakes, jam puffs and whatever other mouth-watering fare Mr Whincup had in mind. I loved to watch him kneading and shaping the dough into loaves, which would then be put aside to 'prove' in tins of various sizes, placed on the flat end of a 'peel' and slid into the huge ovens. Using this long, unwieldy tool was a craft in itself, but the old baker made it look deceptively easy. So easy, in fact, that one morning I remarked that I wouldn't mind having a go, just when a batch was about to be retrieved from the oven. Without a word he handed me the peel, and I gingerly pushed it into the gaping, black oven. What hit me first, full in the face, was a staggering blast of heat. I struggled to persuade a couple of tins to perch on the peel, but they obstinately refused to cooperate, seemingly imbued with a life of their own. Off they shot to the far end of the oven, knocking over most of the other tins like skittles in their flight. Sweat was pouring from my forehead, trickling down my neck – and worst of all, what would Mr Whincup think? The answer to that was hardly what I expected as, pausing for breath, I heard stifled giggles, and turned to catch him and Kath doubled up in silent mirth. At last he took pity on me, grasped the peel from my hot, sticky hands and with a flick of his wrists, had the batch out in no time. I sheepishly returned to my washing-up, pondering on the old soldier's maxim: Never volunteer.

My first important step up came when I was put in charge of the doughnuts. I had cut the mixture into portions with the help of a bun divider, and Kath then showed me how to mould them into shape and space them out on trays to prove. There was a large pan permanently fixed over a couple of strips of gas flames, with a mesh grill at the bottom on which the doughnuts could be removed from the fat and drained. At first I was scared of burning my fingers – so I dropped in the doughnuts, two at a time, from a great height instead, and burned my arms with splashing fat instead. That resulted in some painful blisters, but from then on I always went as near as possible to the oil before letting go. It took a little while for the doughnuts to cook, and I had to stand there with a short stick, turning them over at intervals. They would then come out of the fat on the grill, and I'd leave them to drain for a few minutes before rolling them in caster sugar and arranging them on a greaseproofed wooden tray. It was for Mr Whincup to perform the final task of filling them with jam or cream. They used to say you could always tell somebody who worked in a chip shop a mile off, and it was obviously the same with people in the doughnut business. If I had to go out into town on an errand the shop girls would see me coming, hold their noses and shout: 'Look out, here comes old Doughnuts!' One of my tormentors, a girl called Doris, still calls out 'Doughnuts!' whenever she sees me. After nearly fifty years, that's what I call a standing joke.

I shall never forget the time Mr Whincup went off on a week's holiday, leaving Mr Conduit in charge. I suppose such an act would be seen as male chauvinism these days, since there was nothing about him that suggested that he could cope any better than Kath. The problem was, the old chap seemed to relish his promotion, and soon started ordering us around like a sergeant major. One day he told me in no uncertain terms to make my way up into the loft directly above the bakehouse, open up one of the big bags of caster sugar in store there, and pour its contents down a chute leading into one of the mixing bowls. Sure enough, groping my way across the loft, I located a couple of sacks waiting to be opened, and congratulated myself on a job well done as the fine white crystals disappeared down the chute without mishap. By the time I was back downstairs a mass of ingredients, including my vital contribution, was whirling around in the mixer, soon to be transformed into little Viennese cakes. Kath had prepared traysful of paper cases, and it remained only for Mr Conduit to squeeze the mixture into each one through a piping bag. As Kath and I were concentrating on our own jobs, we were only vaguely aware of his mutterings. But then she nudged my arm, and following her gaze, I saw him struggling to coax the mixture out of the bag, sweat pouring down his face. We raised our eyebrows and grinned at each other. Poor old chap, if he couldn't cope with a simple job like that . . .

He was a persevering type, however, and at last, totally exhausted, he declared them ready for the oven. Still mumbling, and with a look of bewilderment on his sweat-streaked face, he was forced to take a seat while waiting for them to bake – but from being dead to the world, he almost lit up like a Roman candle when he eventually saw the results of his efforts. 'Look at these,' he roared. 'I don't know what's happened to them, I'm sure.' I could see his point; instead of being the usual light brown, these Viennese cakes were a rather fetching pale lemon; and if the proof of the pudding is in the eating, then poor old Mr Conduit was on a loser there, too. As soon as the cakes were cool enough to test, he picked one off the tray, took a big bite – and after chewing in silence for a few seconds, leapt for the door and spat the mouthful on the ground. Had he flipped at last? Perhaps not. When he came back he had a very strange look on his face, and it was clear that I was wrapped up in all this, somewhere. 'Joyce,' he said. 'Would you mind showing me where you got the caster sugar from?' And of course I showed him, and of course it was salt, and of course I got called a 'daft ha'porth' for my troubles.

But what next? When Mr Whincup got to hear about this . . . But he never did, because I had completely misjudged dear old Mr Conduit. He smuggled the cakes home for the rest of the week, to feed his goats. Apparently he allowed them a couple every day, to make up their salt intake. Not a word was said to the boss, and I was full of remorse at having so misjudged my old workmate.

I loved my work at the bakehouse, but by now it seemed that I was fated never to stay in one workplace for very long. I had become allergic to flour, not the best of complaints for a baker, but I was relieved when Mr Wintle, the manager of Birts, offered me a job in the cake shop. Kath left the bakery to get married not long after, and my sister Margaret moved in to take her place. I could tell Harry Whincup thought a lot of her, even though he was not one to praise people to their face. We ate together in the bakehouse at dinner time, and she hadn't been working there long when he asked me to keep my eye on a batch of expensive Dundee cakes, which would be ready to be taken out of the oven before he returned from his lunch. Having mastered the peel at last, I did not feel it was a task beyond my abilities.

After we had finished our sandwiches, Margaret made us a cup of tea. It was good to relax like this in the dinner hour, and where better to do so than on a wooden-topped dough bin, with our backs up against the side of a warm oven? So we idled and chattered until our peace was shattered by Mr Whincup's roars of rage as he pounded down the passage and up into the bakehouse. It wasn't like him. What now? We soon found out when he rushed in, flung open the oven doors, and picked up the peel. The room filled with billows of smoke, and a couple of dozen charred Dundees were deposited on to the nearest dough bin tops. I had never heard such swearing, all of it more or less directed at me, and my stomach churned in fright. Of course it was my fault, and I fully deserved to be dressed down. Worse, I knew Mr Whincup had put me in a position of trust, and I had let him down. But as I've said before, he was a fair-minded man at heart, and as I grovelled, his anger subsided and he said some of the remains could be used as fillings for Banbury cakes; they wouldn't be a dead loss, after all. I've also noted that Harry Whincup had an impish sense of humour, and here again the point was proved. From that day on, if he wanted to tease me, all he had to do was call me 'Alfred'.

CHAPTER TWENTY

Smashing Times

It's an ill wind. It's not much fun being told you're allergic to flour, but I enjoyed being back behind the counter, and was lucky to have another good boss in Fred Wintle, who lived over the shop with his wife Mary and their little ones, David and Rosemary. I was alone in the cake shop, but I knew all the grocery people from my bakehouse days, and they always made sure I never felt left out. Fred was much younger than most of my previous bosses, and was very gentle, quiet and courteous in handling his staff. Because of this we always did our best for him, and the customers seemed to like him, too. At that time I was a terrible butterfingers, always dropping something or another. Poor Fred had just begun to go grey when I started there, and by the time I finished he was white.

The wide shop window contained several glass shelves for the cakes. I was warned from the start that they were worth a lot of money, and could not be replaced. Three of them hung in the middle of the window, suspended by rods from the ceiling. They were usually wiped clean with a cloth, but since I was determined to make a good impression, I decided to take them out and give them a thorough wash. The shop was never open before half past nine, by which time the products of the bakery were ready to serve, so I had an hour in which to clean everything and put out the stock. Armed with a bucket of warm, soapy water and a dishcloth, I found it a slow and anxious job to ease those big glass shelves out for cleaning; but clean and dry them I did, with the minutes ticking away, and a queue had formed outside the shop by the time I was fixing the last shelf, the small one at the top, into place. With a sea of faces watching my every move, and feeling ever more pressed for time, I bowed to the inevitable, let the shelf jiggle from my hand and could only leap away in horror as it speared through the other two and left me with a million shards of glass on the window floor. The onlookers clapped and cheered, but not so poor Mr Wintle, who had rushed in on hearing the almighty crash. 'This is it,' I thought. 'It's me for the sack, nothing surer.' But he just helped me clear up the mess, shaking his head in a sorrowful way, and said nothing when I offered to pay for the damage by having something stopped every week out of my wages. In truth, he never said anything much at all about the incident, ever again. But I managed to smash a few more things after that, on a less grand scale, and I only had to walk into the big shop shouting 'Mr Wintle!' for the poor chap to flinch and inquire in a resigned voice: 'What's broke this time?' I don't know how he put up with me for so long.

I was still getting frequent bouts of illness, and any cold I caught would always turn to acute catarrh. Mam and Vi put their heads together and decided that my health might improve with an open-air job, and it wasn't long before an opportunity arose. There was a new Forestry Commission keeper down at Marian's Lodge, Frank Watson. He had taken over from Mr Humphries, who had lived down there with his daughter Lottie. I was persuaded to go down and ask him whether the Commission had any work to offer, and he told me a girl was needed on his beat; I could start as soon as I had worked out my notice at the cake shop. Work out my notice . . . I hated the thought of leaving there, but I could see that it was doing Mam no good worrying about me, so I went in and explained the situation to Fred Wintle. Perhaps, in the light of the trail of breakages, he breathed a secret sigh of relief. But it was a terrible wrench for me to leave a place in which I had made many friends, and been so happy.

While I had been making good money at the plywood factory I had bought a new bicycle, which had cost fifteen pounds at five shillings a week. It was essential for my new job, as were dungarees, which were just right for the work, and very comfortable. To complete the look I wore wellies with the tops turned over, and I carried my food and water for the day in one of Dad's old canvas satchels slung over my back. I had been told to report to Mailscot Lodge, off the beaten track between the Rock Inn and Symonds Yat, down a wide ash path into the woods.

Fred Wintle, assistant Eileen Hudson and Joyce in front of the bakery door at Birts Stores.

Having lived in the area for so long, I knew most of the workers to a greater or lesser extent. There were two sisters, Kath and Ivy Lewis from Edge End, and though I had had little to do with them previously, I soon struck up a friendship with them, Ivy especially. They had been with the Commission for a few years, and were very hard working; at least, Ivy was before she got mixed up with me. The truth was, I could never take the job very seriously, and I am afraid I managed to involve her in more than one scrape. To me it seemed like one long paid holiday all day, out in my beloved woods and surrounded by nature at its best.

A job on my first day was collecting sycamore seeds around Symonds Yat Rock. 'This is the life,' I thought, sauntering around, filling a bag with the dainty wings as the sun danced through the branches overhead. I soon learned that not all our jobs were as light as this. One of our tasks was to cut briars and weeds from around young saplings in the plantations. I had never used a hook before and it took quite a while, and the sacrifice of a few little trees, before I got the hang of it. We were also expected to clear the browse, the dead branches left behind by the timber felling gangs. This debris was then dragged to a central point and heaped up into a huge bonfire. The resulting clouds of smoke made us all cough and choke, but in the end the wood would dry out and there would be only bright flames round which we'd gather gratefully on our breaks when the days were cold. It wasn't long before I was copying the old hands by toasting my sandwiches over the fire with the aid of a two-pronged hazel stick. Never had food tasted better, even the bits with wood ash and burnt crusts.

Mr Russell was the keeper of the Reddings Lodge at Staunton. I had heard rumours that he hated women, and he certainly didn't like me very much. He was one of those exasperating bosses who expected employees to work for their pay, and he always managed to find me doing something absolutely unconnected with the job in hand whenever he crept up on us while we were on his beat. One morning, during our first ten-minute break, we were all discussing the can-can for some reason. A wide, flat old oak stump gave me an idea; I whispered it to Ivy, her brown eyes crinkled into a grin, and before she knew what she was doing we had launched into our version of the dance, prancing around on the tree stump and kicking as high as we could in our wellies. For the grand finale we turned our backs on our wildly jeering audience and wiggled our dungaree-clad bottoms. We were still in fits of giggles when it dawned on us that nobody else was. Members of our audience had melted away and were all earnestly engrossed in their work – all except one, who stood there with folded arms and not a flicker of amusement on his stern face. He looked pointedly at his watch, which by this time showed that our break had been over for a good fifteen minutes, and we both felt very foolish. Not a word was said. Giving me a look of utter disgust, he jerked his head in the direction of our hooks, and stalked off. But it was no coincidence when Ivy and I were split up the very next day.

I was sent to work on the Sheep's Walk, a lonely stretch of plantation where Mam and I had gone blackberrying some years before. There was no blackberrying that week. The willowherbs and brambles were thick and tough, taller than me, and I worked there like never before for those few days. Obviously, though, my efforts were not enough to satisfy Mr Russell. My next pay packet contained a curt note to the effect that my services would no longer be required. I can't say I was surprised at the time, and looking back now, I suppose I got what I had deserved; what the Commission could never take away was the happy memories of the good friends I'd made while wielding a hook on its behalf.

CHAPTER TWENTY-ONE

Something in the City

For all my bravado, being sacked by the Forestry Commission was a blow to my self-esteem. My boss Frank Watson had been on sick leave at the time, and it cheered me somewhat that my workmates had complained to him about my treatment, and he had not been unsympathetic; but that was all water under the bridge, and the plain fact was that I was out of work and Mam needed my contribution to the housekeeping. Fortunately, in those days, if you wanted a job, there was always something to be had – which was why, with the mud scarcely dry on my Forestry wellies, I found myself dressed up in Brunswick Road, Gloucester, applying for a job as an assistant in the Co-Op café. The advertisement in the local paper said they needed someone to run a kiosk in the café selling sweets, chocolates and cigarettes. The hours were 8.30 a.m. to 6.30 p.m. weekdays and Saturdays, but with Wednesday half-day and meals and uniform provided. I had often wondered what it would be like to work in a big town, meet new people you hadn't known all your life and have a stake in a corner of the world away from your own back door. First signs were not particularly welcoming, however; when I asked an assistant to show me to the manager's office, she did so with great indifference, and I had no feeling of moral support as she pointed me towards a little room with windows in the corner back towards the rear of the café. I was aware of her eyes on me, and those of half a dozen of her colleagues, as I knocked on the door, but things brightened up when I saw the manager. He introduced himself as Mr Davey, and it registered with me instantly that even leaving aside his smart suit, white shirt and dickie-bow tie, he was tall, slim, dark and quite dishy. That combination also had the effect of making me feel a bit of a country bumpkin, but he soon put me at my ease.

He asked me about my previous jobs, and I felt it wiser not to go too deeply into my most recent one. This was no problem, since he was clearly far more interested in my shop experience, and when he spelled out what the kiosk work would entail, I felt far from daunted. When I told him I thought I would be able to cope, he gave me a searching look and then nodded slightly, as if he had satisfied himself on some score. 'Will you be able to start next week?' he asked. I said I could, and offered to bring along some references. 'That won't be necessary, my dear,' he smiled, shaking my hand.

I don't think Mam knew whether to be pleased or sorry. 'It da zound a nice little job,' she said. 'But it'll be a long day fer tha, o' butt, an' thee't 'ave thic journey twice a day, remember.' She must also have been reflecting that this would be far from the fresh-air job she had so recently decided would be the best for my health. It was only then, when she voiced her reservations, that I put some thought into the hours involved. I would have to be at Five Acres Cross by 7 a.m., and would not get home at night until 8.30; even on the half days it wouldn't be much before 4 p.m. Still, being young and a bit of an optimist, I saw no reason why I should not cope; and it was with thoughts of the thrills and excitements of city life in mind that I found myself waiting at the bus stop the following Monday morning.

The Co-Op café was quite an empire. My circular kiosk was opposite the snack bar, just inside the building's main side door, and it had serving hatches for both shoppers inside and passers-by along the street. A short, dark girl opened the door to me that first morning and fitted me out with a dark green overall with long sleeves and white collar and cuffs. She showed me the stockroom where the cigarettes were stored, along with a cupboard stacked with chocolate bars and sweets. After she had produced a long list of stock needed for the kiosk, she supervised me while I found all the items and put them in a big cardboard box. This would be my first job every morning. It was then a case of stacking and displaying all the goodies in the kiosk, putting the float in the till, opening up and waiting for trade. I looked around my little glass cage, the grey street on one side, the drab café on the other; it was a world away from the Forest.

I gradually settled in, and came to know my regular customers. But I missed the easy camaraderie of my little corner of the world;

most of my workmates, the snack bar attendants and café waitresses, seemed to consider themselves a bit above me, and I often noticed them smirking among themselves when some nugget of broad Forest fell from my lips. I liked only two of them, a tall, willowy blonde called Helen and a little widow who reminded me of my late Auntie Doris, not least because she, too, was lame. She clearly wasn't very well off, and I was horrified to hear one day that on several occasions she had had money stolen from her purse in the staff cloakroom. It could only have been an inside job, so on top of everything else, there was an atmosphere of mistrust and suspicion about the place. I was worried because, as the newest employee, I feared that I might be under scrutiny, especially as I had been taken on without references; in the end there was nothing to do but to confront Mr Davey with my anxieties. 'Nobody's ever made accusations against you, Joyce,' he replied. 'I'm able to tell you now that the culprit has been caught red-handed. She was given instant dismissal, so we can all put this unpleasantness behind us.' That was as may be, but other unpleasantnesses refused to go away.

Barton Fair was always a big day in Gloucester. Visitors surged in from all over the country, and the other staff told me horror stories of the work involved, with customers queueing for snacks and meals all day. They also said the manager had a nasty habit of getting everyone to work late that day, and that he would drop me in at the deep end by giving me a job as a waitress for the evening. It was all true, and I found myself trying to cope with four tables – rushing in and out with soup, trying to do a balancing act with hot plates, mixing the orders and growing more flustered by the minute as the customers all shouted at once. A middle-aged woman called Abbie was the head waitress, a sharp-tongued woman who reminded me of Mrs Wyndham Jones, the vicar of Christchurch's manipulative wife. I was soon in her bad books and on the verge of tears.

As one party left, another tableful took its place. Most were on the merry side, having been doing a round of the pubs for most of the day, but I found this a blessing in disguise. They tended to be more tolerant of mistakes, especially after I had rubbed it in that this was my very first stint of waiting on tables. What did seem to be helping me, too, was the fact that Abbie was very swift to clear all my tables, swooping with her tray almost before I could turn around. Perhaps I had misjudged the old girl after all.

And yet, and yet . . . The other girls had said that if nothing else, I should do well for tips, but it seemed that nothing was coming my way. I put it down to the fact that my customers just happened to be mean, or perhaps it was simply that I was not the kind of waitress anyone would wish to tip. Whatever, it was clear that my luck was about to change, for there in the corner I had a full view of a customer slipping a whole half-crown under his plate at the end of his meal. This was silly money; you could dine handsomely at a place like the Co-Op for less than that. But I wasn't arguing, and I couldn't wait to whip back with an empty tray for the dirty crocks. Then all became clear; Abbie was there before me, and I watched in disbelief as she scooped up the coin and dropped it quickly in her apron pocket. 'What do you do about that?' I asked Helen. 'What can you do?' she shrugged. 'She'll only swear it was her tip, and how can you prove otherwise?' I made sure I was first on the scene after that, and picked up quite a few sixpences and shillings. But lightning never strikes twice, and there were no more half-crowns to be found in the Co-Op café that evening.

Just as Mam had predicted, I began to feel the strain of long hours away from home. I was also upset because there was little time at the end of the day to spend with my new boyfriend, Bob Latham, and it seemed a brilliant idea one week when he suggested that he should meet me in Gloucester on my Wednesday half-day, after which we could look round the shops and take in an early picture show before catching the last bus home. I told him to drop into the café at about 1 p.m., thinking it would be a good chance for him to meet some of my workmates. I was thrilled to see him stroll in in his Humphrey Bogart mac and brown trilby, quite the thing for the smart young chaps of the Forest, and I left one of the waitresses serving him with a cup of tea as I hurried down the corridor, full of plans for the afternoon, to fetch my coat. As I was about to enter the cloakroom I heard voices inside. One of the girls was singing 'Where Did You Get That Hat?', while another was making sheep noises, the townie's traditional jibe against the Forester. I could take no more, and rushing through the door I screamed: 'Who the hell do you think you are, you spiteful buggers? My Bob's worth twenty of your kind. You don't find Foresters pinching money from their mates, or sneering behind their backs. When Mr Davey comes in, you can tell him I won't be coming in here to work again; and damn good riddance to the lot of you.' As I glanced back, I had the satisfaction of seeing them standing there, red-faced and pop-eyed with shock. That was the end of my days of working in the city. It had been an experience, but one I had no wish to repeat.

CHAPTER TWENTY-TWO

In Loving Memory

Dad's health was failing rapidly. The coal dust clogging his lungs was choking him to death, and nothing he took in desperation could ease his suffering for long. He had tried every old remedy known to Foresters: a concoction of Spanish liquorice and linseed, a chest rub of warmed fresh goose grease, a rough herb tobacco of the dried leaves of the coltsfoot, those poverty-stricken little yellow flowers that flourished on the pit slag heaps. He would smoke this mixture until supplies ran out and he was back to his twist.

On top of this he developed prostate problems, and became so ill in the spring of 1948 that Dr Lypiatt persuaded him to go into the infirmary on Bristol Road, Gloucester, for an operation. He shuddered at the idea, but there was no alternative; as for us, we visited him as often as we could afford the bus fare. The infirmary was not the most cheerful of places. Though wishing to see Dad, I dreaded our visits there. I had a strong distaste for the smells of hospitals, and all around Dad were men in much the same condition, some of them seeming little more than skeletons. Dad himself appeared to shrink with each visit, his thin arms black and blue with morphine injections. He hated to see us leave, and would beg Mam to take him home and give him a real dinner and a proper cup of tea again. We were glad he didn't seem to realize how ill he was, and we went along with the fantasy that yes, he'd soon be back with us. It was hard not to burst into tears.

He lingered for a couple of weeks, then lapsed into a coma from which he never awoke. He had not been a perfect husband to Mam, but she was still very upset. As for me, Dad's death was just the first stroke of a double blow from which I took a long time to recover. When I had been bobbing back and forth to visit him in hospital, I would rarely pass the gate of my friend Barbara

Greenaway without her coming out to ask how he was, and her mother would often pass on a quarter of sweets or some fruit to take to him. A couple of days after he died, Barbara was looking out for me to inquire about the funeral arrangements. She was full of sympathy, assuring me that she and her family would be at the burial and gripping my hand warmly, but Barbara being Barbara, she was wearing a blue turban over her curlers, and she couldn't quite hide the fact that she was excited about a special date that evening. As I turned the corner at the end of the lane I glanced back and gave her a final wave – and that was the last I saw of her, for the next day she died of a brain haemorrhage at the age of seventeen.

Everyone in the district was deeply shocked: such a lovely girl, so short a life. Suddenly, I felt almost guilty of grieving for Dad. He had had seventy-eight years of life, and had suffered so much. His funeral was quiet and low-key, with only a few friends and relatives present. In contrast, when we went to Barbara's a couple of days later, there was not an empty pew. My heart went out to her parents and brothers. And for the first time in my life, I wondered how God could be so cruel, taking away such a young, vibrant life, causing so much grief. It made no kind of sense to me at all, and I could find no comfort in anything the preacher said. Looking back, I am sure I was in a state of shock. I would spend hours hidden deep in the woods, trying to come to terms with death. My favourite time was towards evening, letting the peace and calm of nature wash over me. Here was life in abundance – tall trees, quietly growing in stature and beauty, hosts to myriads of little creatures; birds flitting from branch to branch, trilling their last songs before nightfall; tall ferns vying for space with thorny briars; the earth itself teeming with beetles, ants and tiny shoots. I thought of autumn, when everything came to fruition before dying away; then the long sleep of winter, and the wonder of another spring. It began to dawn on me that nothing in nature is wasted, and I would return home feeling much more at peace with myself.

As I've said before, life in the Forest sometimes seemed cheap in those days. Vi's friend and dancing companion Eve Ward was

Eve Ward, with her boys Clive and Roger. Eve died in a tragic accident.

another lovely woman cut down by tragedy. Life for her had not been one long Saturday night at Bicknor Village Hall, and though she worked hard bringing up her three children, she discovered her husband was not as devoted to her as she remained to him. She would never have a word said against him, in spite of his unkindnesses; but nevertheless, their marriage had broken down, and it seemed that divorce was her best chance of seeking a new and happier life. On the day before it was to be made absolute, she was hanging washing out on her wire line. For some reason, perhaps in search of better reception, she had attached a cable to it from her wireless set, and when her hand went up to it to peg up her clothes, she was electrocuted. So another family had to bear pain and grief, along with her friends. Surely there was more to life than this.

Through Shaded Dells

Through shaded dells in childhood days I wandered,
Where soft the mossy paths I trod,
Beneath tall oaks and graceful beech I pondered
The mysteries of life, and death, and God.
At peace among the bluebells in their splendour
I felt his presence reaching out with love,
Across the haze, bright shafts of light so slender
Pierced through that leafy canopy above.
High, high upon a branch, a blackbird sweetly
Poured out his song, as pure as silver bells.
Oh, just once more, to feel again, completely,
That inner peace I found in shaded dells.

CHAPTER TWENTY-THREE

Kismet

Although I had had several boyfriends since parting from my first love, some magic ingredient seemed to be missing. I was impatient to find *the* one, and my instinct refused to let me settle for second best. Not that I suppose that thought was uppermost in my mind that Saturday night I went over to the club at Sling with a few of my old friends from Birts Stores. Still, a good evening was in prospect. One of the most popular bands in the Forest was on the bill, the Rhythm Serenaders, led by Melvyn Case, who at that time was courting poor Barbara Greenaway. It was a great night, but in between being swung around the floor by a succession of partners, I constantly found my gaze wandering towards the musicians – and more particularly, the drummer. He was crashing away with his head bent forward and what I took to be a scowl on his face. 'Coo, yun 'im nice lookin',' I thought. 'Just my type, dark 'an 'andsome, but don' 'im look bloomin' miserable!' I didn't get to speak to him, but the memory lingered.

This was the time of the first flush of the National Health Service, and it was changing people's lives for the better. Those who had been gummy for years were suddenly flashing gleaming new smiles. Folks who had stumbled around in a haze were suddenly the proud possessors of not one pair of spectacles but two, one for reading and the other for long distance. In for a penny, I decided to have all my bad teeth out. I chose McPhail of Lydney, who took out my front teeth first, six in one go, using a light gas he called Twilight Sleep.

I felt so embarrassed that I wouldn't go anywhere for ages, until Mam persuaded me to go with her on a coach trip to the Kemble Theatre in Hereford organized by a local enthusiast, Mrs Parker. We got on at the King's Head in Berry Hill, and as I made my way to my seat, I noticed a dark-haired young man sitting half-way down the aisle. My heart leapt, for this was no mere mortal dark-haired young man. It was the drummer from the Rhythm Serenaders, no

*The Rhythm Serenaders in full swing, with Bob
laying down the beat on drums.*

less, and better still, he was sitting next to a boy I knew. It was Mrs
Parker's brother Jim, and although he had once been my boyfriend,
we had parted on good terms and it wasn't long before he was
turning round in his seat offering me a Player's Weight. For the
first time in my life, I didn't have much to say. I was too busy
trying to disguise my lack of teeth with a silk scarf. Bob Latham,
the drummer, told me years later that his first, misleading
impression of me was of a quiet, shy little girl with wrinkled
stockings. He'd even noticed that; the truth was, one of my
suspenders had somehow come adrift, and I had fled off the bus at
Hereford, hoping nobody would notice, in a desperate rush to carry
out emergency repairs in the ladies'. I had heard of a trick using a
sixpenny bit to replace the lost suspender button, and thank
goodness, it worked.

I've no idea what the show was at the Kemble. What I do know is that when the comedian came on, I kept glancing over to Bob to see how he reacted to the jokes. It was uncanny; if he was roaring with laughter, so was I; some jokes might be getting a big reaction from the audience, but only a slight smile from us two. I pondered on this on the sleepy coach on the way home, and after we had said our goodbyes to the rest at the King's Head, Mam and I walked home for a welcome cup of tea. 'I've met the man I'm going to marry, tonight, Mam,' I told her as we sat by the kitchen fire. She looked rather startled, and there was sarcasm in her voice when she asked: 'Who's the lucky man, then, o' butt?'

'That chap Bob Latham, who was with Jim,' I replied. He didn't know it, but his fate had been sealed, poor man.

Coleford Cinema had been closed for a while for redecoration, and though I was longing to see what they'd done, I couldn't afford to go. A chap had been pestering me to go out with him for ages, and when he asked me again shortly after the reopening, I amazed him by saying 'yes'. I said I particularly wanted to see the film on that week, so for the price of a ticket, some chocolates and an ice cream in the interval, I graciously allowed him to hold my hand on the back row of the one-and-nines. He offered to walk me home afterwards, but as I lived in Berry Hill, and he in Broadwell, I insisted on catching the Blue and White bus. He'd served his purpose as far as I was concerned, and that was the end of it.

The pubs were turning out as the bus pulled in, and my heart jumped when I saw Bob and Jim joining the queue. I picked a seat not too far from the door, hoping Bob would see me as he stepped aboard, and it worked perfectly. He was soon squeezing into the seat next to me, and from then on my only problem was that the bus was speeding along all too quickly for my liking. I had my top set of teeth by then, and although they still felt like a tea tray in my mouth, I was by no means as shy and retiring as he had found me the last time. I expected him to get off at Five Acres, where he lived, but to my joy he stayed on with me to the King's Head. When we got off, he asked me to see him again the following week, and it wasn't hard to say 'yes'. I ran down the lane bubbling over with excitement.

Bob Latham at the time he met Joyce.

It was a long wait until the following Friday, and doubts began to creep in. He was Jim's friend, I had finished with Jim – were they cooking up some act of revenge between them? We were going to Monmouth Pictures, and he had promised to be at the bus stop. I started getting ready hours before it was time to go, and irritated Mam by asking repeatedly whether I looked all right. A dash up the lane, just as head-over-heels as the one in the opposite direction the previous week – and then a plop of my heart as I realized he was nowhere to be seen. I could hear the bus approaching and I was at a loss to know what to do, I felt so sick with disappointment. A few other passengers were waiting, and it was only when the last one was stepping aboard that Bob came dashing round the corner, flushed but on time – just. We had a lovely evening, with so many more to follow; and though true love did not run smoothly all the time, after the flaming rows, usually my fault, it was great to kiss and make up. We frequently went for long walks in my beloved woods, more often than not with his good-natured Alsatian Laird. That poor dog must have been relieved when we married, because at the end of our walks he could never decide which one of us he should follow home. He'd trot behind me half-way up the lane, then chase after Bob – and though Bob always won, Laird only seemed really happy when we both went the same way home together. To tell the truth, so was I.

Bob's home at Five Acres Cross, fronting the main road, was very different from our little bungalow. Though he shared it only with his father, it had four bedrooms, four rooms downstairs and any number of outhouses, too. Such was the tight-knit nature of the Forest, I suppose I should not have been too surprised to learn that Bob and I were second cousins – but in fact I was shocked, and remained so until I was reassured that our marriage prospects remained unharmed. His mother Irene, or Rene as she was known, was the daughter of my great uncle Bill Farr, the result of an extra-marital liaison between him and an unknown girl; Bill was the brother of my grandfather, the man who had brought me up as my Dad. Bill's wife Alice could not have children, so the couple adopted Rene and Alice brought her up as her own daughter. I have often thought about this remarkably generous gesture, one that would have been completely beyond me.

Bob had an elder brother Jack, a very popular chap. Their mother Rene died when Bob was nine, but she had been an invalid through acute asthma for several years before that. Bob's only memory of her is as a weak figure lying in bed, unable to lift a finger. Young Jack, five years older than the man who became my husband, managed most of the housework, as well as acting almost as a mother to his little brother. After Rene's death the family managed as best it could, with good neighbours rallying round. There were the Thorntons and an old lady just across the road known by Bob as Aunt Polly, but there were others, too, all lending a hand from time to time. Jack started work at fourteen at the Red and White paper shop at Coleford, later to be one of my haunts, and his delivery round took him past a gypsy camp at Staunton Green. Realizing that none of them had been taught the

Bob (left) outside his home at Five Acres with his brother Jack and friend Trevor Jones.

three Rs, he would stop every morning to read them the main news story, and this has often struck me since then as a wonderful gesture from such a young boy. They say the good die young, and that has never been truer than in the case of Jack. His journey to work took him down Sparrow Hill, at that time the main road into Coleford from the Berry Hill area, and he had been at the paper shop for about five months when his bike collided with a truck one morning and he was killed outright. It was almost a year to the day after his mother's death, and Bob's father went mad with grief, smashing the cycle to pieces. What's more, he withdrew into himself, leaving the little boy very much to his own devices. Not even the massive show of support for the family at the funeral could cut through Mr Latham's grief. Bob still has a sheaf of letters of condolence and he recalls that there were almost unprecedented scenes when Jack's friends the gypsies turned up at the church to pay their last respects.

So it was a lonely childhood for poor Bob in that big house from then on. There were of course shafts of light. His cousin Bill was a good pal, as was a boy called Trevor Jones, and when his father went out to seek out company at the Rising Sun, the landlady Mrs Byatt would let Bob play in the kitchen for an hour or two until it was time for them to go home. Later, Bob threw himself into sport, playing rugby for several Forest clubs at different times; and of course there was the drumming, self-taught with the help of the big band music that was forever on the wireless in those days.

His Auntie Crink Ennis, his father's sister, did most to help him over the loss of his mother and Jack – but here again, the story was ultimately tragic. Her husband Ralph had been in poor health for years, but she was still devastated when he died. She struggled on for a while, kept going by the need to keep an eye on her elderly mother, who lived in Cannop; but inevitably, the old lady, too, eventually passed away, and not long afterwards poor Crink was found drowned in a tub of rainwater beside her house, and suicide was the only verdict the coroner could pass. My childhood was tough, there's no doubt about that; but I often think how lucky I was when I compare it with Bob's lonely, tragedy-filled young life.

CHAPTER TWENTY-FOUR

The Lathams

Over the years I have pieced together a smattering of the Lathams' family history. Bob never said a lot about his childhood, and when I learned more about it, I began to understand why. His paternal grandfather John started life at Coalway, on the Coleford road opposite Ludlam's Farm in the meadows. By sheer coincidence, one of his descendants, David Latham, has lived there for a few years with his wife Joan and their family, though the house has been much enlarged and improved.

Grandfather John and his wife had eight children. One died young, and they were left with four boys and three girls: Bob's father Bill, Tom, Fred, who was killed in the First World War, Jack, Annie, Alice and Mary, better known as Crink. I have been told that John Latham was well known as a horse doctor, and people would come from miles to visit him when one of their animals was sick. If the horse was too ill to move, he would go along and treat it on the spot. Bob still has some grand old textbooks of his, as well as his own tried and trusted remedies.

Bob's father Bill inherited this talent, and worked with horses in the Bix Head quarries. His team had the dangerous task of shifting huge slabs of stone from the quarry to the stonemason's yard down Fetter Hill, a long, hard journey through the woods by way of a dram road. He had also worked and owned freeminers' gales, and operated a milk round. His last pony, Tommy, was much loved by local children, some of whom were sometimes allowed to ride him. One of Tommy's greatest fans was Brian Raymond, who now runs a clothing store in Coleford. The pony could also be seen trotting proudly between the shafts of Bill's trap from time to time. Like many Foresters, Bob's father also kept a flock of sheep as a sideline, creatures that wandered the common by day but were always penned in one of his fields at nightfall. It was often Bob's job to search them out and round them up with the help of a collie dog

Old Grandfather and Grandmother Latham with baby Barbara Sangers at Cannop.

called Dusty, and he was also expected to lend a hand at lambing, shearing and dipping. There was no arguing with Bill Latham; he was very strict with Bob, and did not believe in sparing the rod. It reflected the way he had been brought up, and he was not the only old Forester to be a hard taskmaster. For all that, Bob would never hear a word said against him, and they loved each other in their own undemonstrative way.

Bob's grandmother must have had a handful, with all those children to bring up, feed and clothe. Alice went into service when she left school and married a Londoner, George Sangers. Annie and her husband Lewis Joseph, a local man, emigrated to an only partly tamed Canada, worked hard and brought up lots of children, descendants of whom are now scattered through that vast country. Annie lived long, and we always exchanged greetings at Christmas, a tradition we uphold with her now elderly daughter Nancy. As I have mentioned, Fred died in the First World War, while Tom remained single all his life and stayed in his parents' home.

*Bill Latham and Cedric Wood with a horse team hauling stone at
Broadwell Quarry.*

The only one who caused his mother real heartache was Jack. He
found work in a slaughterhouse in Lydney after leaving school, and
they say he was doing well there until one day when he made a
costly mistake. A freshly slaughtered carcase had been left on the
floor for his attention, but somehow he forgot about it until all its
meat had turned bad. Terrified of the consequences, he felt the only
thing to do was run away from home – which he did by smuggling
a few odds and ends of his belongings out of the house, dashing
across the meadows to Coleford railway station and eventually
fetching up in Blackpool. His parents were frantic with worry,
especially his poor mother, but from that day, he never once
contacted them or anyone else in the Forest.

His heartbroken mother lit an oil lamp every night and placed it
in the window as a beacon for his return. It glowed through the
gloom for years and years, but Jack never saw it. She clung to the
hope of seeing him again until the day she died, and only then was
the lamp extinguished forever. As for the rest of them, they believed

that if some tragic accident had not befallen Jack, there was every hope that he might still be alive in another country. This was a family, after all, with first-hand knowledge of transatlantic emigration. What threw them completely, when Bob's father was nearly sixty, was an advertisement placed in a national newspaper by one A. Latham of Blackpool. Did any Lathams still live in the Forest of Dean? it asked. If so, could they please contact the advertiser?

Bill wrote off wanting to know more – and when a letter with a Blackpool postmark returned a few days later, the mystery of Jack's disappearance was solved at last. A. Latham was Jack's widow Annie, only recently bereaved. All the time they had been married he had never once mentioned his origins, and steadfastly refused to do so; the only clue had been when she found some reference to the Forest among his effects. They had had three children who had grown up never knowing their paternal grandparents, and now they had all married and started families of their own.

Bill was upset that Jack had died without the chance of a reunion, but the solving of the mystery seemed to give him some relief. He was also intrigued to meet his brother's family – and you could say he hit it off with his widow Annie, because the outcome was that he eventually married her, bringing her back to a very different way of life in the Forest. It was a confusing time for Bob. His new-found aunt was suddenly his stepmother, his cousins his step-brothers and sister, their children no longer his second cousins but his nephews and nieces. Trying to explain it all to outsiders still brings me out in an itchy rash.

Bob got on well with his step-brothers, Alec and Jack, who had followed their father into butchery. He liked his step-sister Doris, too, though he saw her less often. One great bonus of having a newly discovered family in Blackpool became clear when holiday time came around, and Bob usually stayed with Jack when he had a week's holiday. Jack in particular took to the Forest and Foresters, and they took to him. His wife Evelyn couldn't get over our outside loos and easy-going way of life, after the bustle of Blackpool. She had worked as a barmaid most of her life, much of the time at the Tower, and was quite taken by our quiet little pubs. It was Jack's brother Alec, though, who went the whole hog and

*Bob Latham as
a baby, with his
parents and
brother Jack.*

moved down here to his father's birthplace. He and his wife
Winnie and their children stayed at Five Acres for a while,
although their eldest son John was away doing his National Service
for most of this time. Bob's father was particularly fond of the
youngest boy, David, who suffered from asthma. Alec later took on
the stewardship of a local club, but Winnie was less able to settle
in the south, and returned to Blackpool for a while with their
young daughter, another Winnie.

So it was that the big, quiet house at Five Acres became the hub
of activity for a while, with all kinds of family members who had
so recently been strangers coming and going. It was perhaps not
surprising that Bill's new wife Annie, well over sixty, succumbed
to homesickness on several occasions, and had spells back in her
beloved Blackpool before returning to the Forest once more. Bob's
father died a year before our marriage, but by this time Annie had
got more used to the ways of the Dean, and stayed down here until
she, too, passed away and made her last journey to a resting place
by the sea. It didn't stop Jack, Evelyn and their daughter Joan
continuing to visit us, and we went to see them, too, when money
allowed, taking our children in later years. They were good-hearted
people and I felt happy for Bob, finding a new family in such a
bizarre way after a childhood of loneliness.

CHAPTER TWENTY-FIVE

Fond Farewells

After my stormy departure from the Co-Op café, I was on the labour market once again. I had written off any wages due to me, and was pleasantly surprised when they arrived, along with a letter from head office. In it, the chief cashier offered me a position in his department, and I was pleased that my handling of the till money and the little bit of office work I had done in connection with the kiosk stock had met with his approval. The job he was offering would have meant more money and shorter hours, but it still added up to a long day; besides, office work had no appeal for me.

Instead, I was lucky enough to find a job at Les Ellis' grocery store at Mile End, about ten minutes' bike ride from my home. He was not very tall, with sharp features and an equally sharp turn of phrase. Happily, he was often out and about with orders, leaving the shop to me and Frances Kear, the other assistant. Frances was a few years older than me, one of those unmarried sisters of a large family who ended up looking after her mother. She had been at the shop from before Mr Ellis took over, and was a model of neatness and efficiency with her immaculately waved greying curls, spotless overalls and crisp, white blouses. It was a busy little shop, and I found the Mile End folk cheerful and friendly. One of the younger customers was Joyce Smith, a grammar school girl who used to pop in on errands for her mother. I particularly enjoyed a chat with her, little knowing that we would become close friends, bringing up our families together and sharing in each other's joys and sorrows.

One morning there was a torrential thunder storm, with rain beating so hard on the corrugated zinc roof that we could hardly hear ourselves speak. Lightning flashed across the shop window, and thunder boomed and rumbled. Just when I thought it was easing it came on with a new ferocity, and as I watched the water streaming down the road like a river, I grew increasingly anxious.

I kept thinking of Mam, all alone down the lane, and hoped desperately that the water wasn't flooding down it like it sometimes did. Mr Ellis was working in his little office, and I had just made up my mind to ask him whether I could call back home when I saw Dr Tandy hurrying up the steps. My heart turned over, because I knew instantly that he was not calling in for a quarter of sweets.

He stepped straight up to me and said: 'I think you'd better get along home straight away, my dear. Your mother's had another heart attack, and I'm sending for an ambulance to take her into hospital as soon as possible.' My stomach lurched with fear as I rushed home, but I had already missed the ambulance. Vi was there, and explained that water had gushed down the lane and through the front gate, and Mam had been trying to keep it out of the house with a hard broom when the exertion proved too much. She had collapsed face-down in a pool of water by the gate – but by some miracle, Barbara Greenaway's elder brother Ken had had trouble with his works' van that morning. He had decided to try it out down the lane, something he had never done before, and he had noticed Mam as he passed our gate. A few more minutes and she would have drowned.

It meant another long stay for her in hospital, six weeks, and Mr Ellis was very good when I needed time off to visit her; he never stopped any money out of my wages, either. Uncle Bill, her son, was still working away, but he came home to visit Mam and told me to be on the lookout for a different house, somewhere less isolated and nearer Coleford. I did as he said, and tracked down a little end-of-row cottage half-way down Lords Hill. It wasn't a palace, by any means, but it was in Bill's price range, and its amenities included a flush toilet downstairs, two bedrooms and a boxroom that Bill said he would convert into a bathroom. Best of all, it had electricity and running water.

Moving day, which I was dreading, deep down, came all too quickly for me, but I was glad for Mam's sake. Bob's father had kindly lent us his pony Tommy and his trap, and it was surprising how much could be loaded on – not that Bob would overload it, for Tommy's sake. We owned very little furniture, but it was a

The Lathams' pony Tommy, which was aged over thirty when he died.

shock to discover how many bits and pieces we had accumulated over the years. I hung back when the last load disappeared down the lane. The bungalow already looked deserted, and a terrible feeling of sadness crept over me. This was where I had spent so many happy years, and it was an aching wrench to have to leave. I spent a few minutes in each room, memories crowding into my mind. I peeped through my tiny bedroom window, where the larch tree brushed against the panes and the sticky red cones were within hand's reach in the spring. Then I carefully closed and locked the doors for the last time.

I could hear the clop of Tommy's hooves as I drew the gate behind me. Bob was waiting patiently down the lane, but I allowed myself just one last backward glance as I hurried towards him. The house seemed to stare back reproachfully. 'Goodbye, happy years,' I thought. 'Goodbye, beautiful woods. You will always mean home to me.'

CHAPTER TWENTY-SIX

New Beginnings

It took a while for us to get used to our new home. Steep hills mean low gears, and the traffic thundering up and down the road kept us awake at first. Water at the turn of a tap was a real joy, though the 'corporation pop' didn't taste nearly as sweet as our sparkling spring-well water. I also latched on quickly to the joys of electricity, but poor old Mam was scared stiff of it, and we had a terrible job trying to convince her that she would not be electrocuted when she switched on. In fact she still insisted on taking her old candlestick and candle up to bed with her. The electric iron Bob bought me proved to be a mixed blessing, too. Of course, Mam refused to use it, so I found myself doing the bulk of the ironing each week while she did bits and pieces with her flat irons, which she warmed on the front-room range. She had brought her three cats with her, buttering their paws on the first night to stop them wandering off. I was scared they would get run over, but they soon established a territory in the back gardens, and saw no need to cross the road.

Bob's father had died, I was much easier in my mind about Mam, so at last it was time to start making wedding plans, after a three-year engagement. Living accommodation posed no problem, since Bob insisted that we should live in his family home. I dearly wanted to start married life with some new clothes, and towels, bed linen, china and pots and pans I could call my own, but the problem, as always, was lack of funds. In search of more pay, I left Ellis' store and started work at the cable works at Lydbrook, in the stranding department. My fear of machinery was not eased when I was confronted by a long, clanking monster in which seven bobbins of wire whirled around at a terrific speed. The wires fed out at the other end twisted together into a single thick strand, after which they were rolled automatically around large wooden cylinders. My job would be to keep a close watch on the bobbins, in case the thin wire should snap. It often did, and my task then was to heat a soldering iron over a blowlamp and rejoin the broken strands.

The next strander was worked by a no-nonsense, witty blonde girl called Betty Roberts. She had been there for years, and I watched in humble admiration as she deftly handled her machine, which always seemed to run more smoothly than mine. She was quite an expert at hairdressing, and often she would casually load up the machine, shout across for one of the men to keep an eye on it, and then go off to the cloakroom to fix somebody's locks. Nothing ever seemed to go wrong when she was away; her obedient bobbins spun sweetly without a hitch, while mine would develop multiple fractures if I so much as blinked.

This led me to the conclusion that I was not machinery-minded. Strangely, the foreman was fast reaching the same point of view, and I was pleased when another post fell vacant at the factory, this time in the far more familiar territory of the canteen. All the workers bought differently priced tickets for their meals, and the job advertised involved issuing these from a combined till-cum-ticket dispenser. I took the Co-Op head cashier's letter along to the interview, and that was enough to land me the job. I already knew the canteen supervisor, a Berry Hill girl called June White, and soon made friends with the rest of the staff. When my services were not required on the ticket machine I helped out in the kitchen, washing up or peeling vegetables. As a free cooked meal was part of the deal, Mam was saved the bother of cooking for me in the evening; and endless cups of tea on tap made this the kind of job I could really enjoy.

Meanwhile, our wedding plans were progressing slowly. I ordered my dress from Ivor Griffiths in Coleford, where I had been a customer since starting at the Red and White paper shop, and I was thrilled when he made a present of a full-length veil to go with it. The staff, including an ex-Bell's Grammar School mate, Pauline Morgan, and her colleague Mrs Butler, clubbed together to present me with a lovely tablecloth and a pile of towels and tea cloths.

My bridesmaids were to be my cousin Wendy and my half-sisters Margaret, Eileen and little Yvonne. I chose pale turquoise

*Bob's stepmother Annie with
Joyce in the 1950s.*

material for the older girls, and pale mauve for the smaller ones.
All Bob had to get was a new suit, shirt and shoes – but who looks
at the bridegroom, anyway? My Uncle Bill was to give me away,
and he kept saying he couldn't wait. Bob's best man was to be his
step-brother Jack from Blackpool; the wedding would be at
Christchurch, followed by a reception at the King's Head, where
the landlady Ann Lewis and her daughter Doreen would do the
catering. As for the date, we hadn't even forgotten to arrange that.
It would be 25 September 1954.

Bob entrusted me with his mother's beautiful gold locket – but
only until I had a daughter, when it would be passed on to her.
Sure enough, our girl Sally wore it on her wedding day. Vi lent me
a bracelet, so I had something old, something new and something
borrowed; but something blue? Enough of Mam's superstitious

nature had rubbed off on me to prompt me to go out and buy half a yard of blue ribbon, and while Bob was out carousing the night away with his friends and male relatives, I was sitting in our front room painstakingly sewing little blue bows to my white knickers.

My thoughts that evening were a mixture of excitement and sadness, and I don't suppose I was the first bride to have felt that way. On the one hand, a brand new life awaited me; on the other, I hated to think of Mam left on her own. She had been the centre of my world for so long, and now someone else was taking her place. I longed to tell her how much I loved and appreciated her, that last night, but the words stuck in my throat. I knew that if I started, we'd both end up bawling our eyes out; so I kissed her goodnight, as usual, and rushed up to my bedroom where I put all my feelings down in a long letter.

A long way from the Forest: Joyce and Bob on a day trip to London.

When it was finished, I sealed it in an envelope and propped it up on my dressing table, where she would be sure to see it. With the writing of that letter, the feelings of guilt seemed to slip away, and my thoughts turned positively to the new life ahead of me. Tomorrow, little Joycee Farr would be gone, and in her place would be a fully grown woman, sharing the ups and downs of life with her new husband. I had faced new beginnings before, but nothing that would change my destiny like this great adventure.